PROPHETS

OTHER POETRY BY KWAME DAWES

Resisting the Anomie
Progeny of Air
Prophets
Jacko Jacobus
Requiem
Shook Foil
Mapmaker
Midland
New and Selected Poems
Bruised Totems
I Saw Your Face
Wisteria
Brimming
Impossible Flying
Gomer's Song
Hope's Hospice
Back of Mount Peace
Wheels
Duppy Conqueror
City of Bones

With John Kinsella
Speak from Here to There
A New Beginning

PROPHETS

KWAME DAWES

PEEPAL TREE

First published in Great Britain in 1995
Reprinted in 2003
New edition, 2018
Peepal Tree Press Ltd
17 King's Avenue
Leeds LS6 1QS
England

ISBN 9781845234041

Supported using public funding by
ARTS COUNCIL
ENGLAND

but it was something to have at least a choice of nightmares

Joseph Conrad

ACKNOWLEDGEMENTS

Special thanks to Robert Gibbs for his enthusiastic
encouragement about this poem.

For Lorna, Sena and Kekeli
and for
those who have walked the Road with me.

CONTENTS

PART THREE

PART FOUR

PROLOGUE

To write her I construct enigma
in my leaping metaphors, for the
poem dictates its own logic and

mystery. I have an investment
in this tale – she is the prophetess
whose finger, pointed, stirred bumps

on my flesh; she is the voice that
spoke my name while I sat, eyes closed
in the congregation, secure as

victim, broke and hungry as never
before, my stomach growling;
maybe it was the cake of tears

in my eye-corner that she saw,
or the sway of my broken body
which made her prophesy my need,

but the miracle of gifts offered,
the promise of a meal and debts paid,
made doubt a sin of ingratitude.

It is this my priestess of the pure,
whose eyes I dared not look into
for fear that my constant indiscretions

would be seen and revealed,
this daughter of holiness who fell
so impossibly hard into the thighs

of unbelievers, it is she whose poem
now translates itself here. And I
confess my reluctance to let her go

as she was, blue dress and white head-tie
in the corner of the room,
with a soft voice that never

lifted beyond the drab monotone,
whose every movement was a sign.
Here, in yet another

of my squalid indiscretions,
having forgotten the overwhelming
sweetness of control over the elements,

the dialogue with the supernatural,
having forgotten the security
of sinlessness, the sure path

of daily guidance of the spirit
turning in my head – turn left
or right, go forward or back –

here, in this barren city of silence,
I reach for her tarnished flesh,
pull back, afraid to be found out,

and then dare to imagine her coupling
in the blackness of the beach,
her coming, that same mouth

saying, “Harder, harder, harder.”
I am seeking clues, some explanation
that will reveal the sleight-of-hand

of this fundamentalist miracle,
something to make me look
better than a gullible fool.

And yet, from a ladder in the clouds,
her memory descends mysterious
and miraculous in its detail.

This poem shapes its own peculiar metaphors,
its own demanding regimen of faith,
and Clarice the prophetess glows the more.

I know now that she did have wings,
brilliant multicoloured plumes
that lifted her above the squalor and muck.

PART ONE

CHAPTER I

Introit

Goats chewing almond seeds
daub their sweat into the pale blue wall;
they scamper from the congregation coming

in a wave of perfumes and too much cologne,
in casual brights and patent leather,
bibles tucked like swords under their arms.

Clarice's make-up is minimal; the mascara
thin under the red eyelid. She is in
reverie. The visions are already spinning.

In her blue chiffon dress and white head-tie,
she carries her virgin body like a saint,
the prayers turning in her bright morning eyes.

It is the journey there that torments her,
through the poverty and squalor beyond the wall
separating this hibiscus-red avenue from the shack

and shingle of the spreading ghettos
where her father's dust-worn blackness fades
into the shadow and grey of the smoke yards.

Head forward, it is the reaching only that she sees.
Her mantle of importance is her light. "Good mornings"
are guarded; the brothers keep their righteous distance.

The slick “off-the-wharfs” car breathes in Sunday morning’s
blossoming. Poinsettias bleed
on the riot of green. It is the birthing season,

and pregnant sisters pray for a Christmas baby.
The brothers who have come to pick her up
and carry her to the gathering know she will

flail them with her revelations of their straying souls,
so no foul imaginings enter their fertile minds
on the slow drive through Kingston’s satellite suburbs.

Clarice stands in the spill of shade and light
of the sprawling mango trees which darken the old grey
cement, the leaning tombstone of the Castleberrys,

white landed aristocrats with their St. Andrew
lilt of an accent, who called their souls
Jamaican years before the slaves had Africa ripped

from their dreamings and heaven flights.
Sunday strolls casual as this magic of ghosts
wavering in the light dispersal of seed.

The brothers recite their verses to ward off
the lust, seeing Clarice like that, her curve of breast
and wet, dipped lips, the glow of moistness

on her ochre soft face. The rolled-down windows
temper the bite of her perfume, and the car noses
silent through the wrought gates, into the city’s

Sunday dream. All in silence past the
antennae of steel and babel metal of the madman's
shrine on Hope Road, they eye his red daze

and say a prayer for his tormented soul. Too late
now to stop for the casting out of demons; the congregation
is waiting, and Clarice is never late.

ii

The gravel driveway is strewn with goats'
droppings of olive green and black;
cane trash sucked dry-dry and coconut husks

litter the parking lot, spilling from the grilled
doorway of the Guild Building. In the air the stale renk
of spilt Red Stripe, curdling vomit, ganja and

sweat is thick as in the drifting carcass of an old slaver
after the liberation of the encumbered souls.
This is the hangover of Saturday night's rites of carnival

release before the righteous glare of Sunday penance:
that slow deliberate march to the chapel door
where the congregation rocks its own lamentations.

Inside, the tiles are slippery with brown glass sparkling
under the swelling sun, frothing Guinness and a yellowed
sea of spilled curried goat. Shifting mountains

of flies dance around the gnawed remains
of boiled flesh and bones, the finely grained white
rice. The goats bleat their remembrances in the yard.

Before long, the hallelujah chorus will startle
this stale cloud of carnival and the sweep of prophecies
will clear the air. With new intoxications, the congregation

will wheel and tambourine away the yawning spirits
who have overslept, hungover like this, wincing at the scream
in the electric air, the knocking of the fans

dangerously turning above the clapping and singing.
Clarice picks her way through the debris of sin
and bows in prayer while the brothers broom

the mess into mounds to be burned: pyres of sacrifice
turning in the morning air. Then, singing softly,
Clarice sirens the gathering to its worship.

CHAPTER II

In a Shady Cloister Mew'd

Often before bed and the ritual of preparation,
she meets Castleberry's horny ghost in the chilled
living room, staring her down with a boldness

he never had in life, as if this lusting
is the essence of his otherwise proper
Church-of-England, community-leader character.

Dead now, with no certain home,
he indulges his ability to walk through
the thick plastered walls

to stare at the half-dressed softness
of this woman. Clarice is used to the company
and feels his loneliness. She does not

turn him out into the abyss; he is old,
means no harm, only wants to look, no touching.
The room smells of earthworms and dank soil.

He does not talk much, instead he watches
with the soft appreciative eye of an old dead lover
there in the corner, where sometimes he startles her

with his sly presence. She says goodnight,
tossing her waist like her mother would,
just for his pleasure, and maybe to see if you lose the

fluidity of the pelvis in the solid air
of prophecy and salvation. Laughing softly,
she feels the looseness in her thighs.

On *Hawaii Five O* reruns, the boys sweat brown,
rippling their humping bodies over the frothing sea,
their paddles parting, dipping, withdrawing, horning

the cut and turn of the ocean. The girls
turn their raffia leaves into whips,
as the horns ejaculate into the tropic green.

Clarice tightens the Ponds' lid, feeling the soft
caress of the cream cooled in the light breeze.
Her face is white in the ornate mirror.

The prophecy comes without announcement.
She gets them on the toilet seat sometimes.
This time it is in her mirror. She squints to see.

Christ with thick, dipped-in-burnt-sienna lips
and an insanity of locks leans against the wind.
Below, the hogs graze with cleft hoof and snout

there on the rocks of Gaderenes. Silent in the bland
Sabbath morning, the villagers lock their doors,
garlic hanging like blown light bulbs to ward

off the unknown with its sharp stink. For the
madman is back, skipping through the streets,
manacles ripping into open sores on his skin.

Hungry, he howls through the night,
leaping the rocks to meet Jesus, the pastoral dread,
swallowing the seascape in his waiting.

The poor unsuspecting hogs sprint blind into the
chop of the sea; the demons gasp for air,
the salt consuming their machinations;

and the fishermen dip and draw their paddles,
their brown naked backs sweating with salt spray
and the exertion of humping over this liquid shrine,

the scarless wound of a miracle. On the beachhead, Clarice
stands waiting for their coming with the froth
and white of the sea against the black sand at her feet.

Clarice seines from this bounty of her dreaming –
this swelling of her breasts naked behind her too hot
robe, from this miracle of the healed man's mind,

from the rattling sticks of the tropical drums,
the hula girls with the fluid hips and raffia, from
the eyes of Castleberry gentle on her thigh –

the voice of her saviour breaking the erotic twilight.
She stores this vision in her heart for the morning service.
She notices the breakthrough of her sweat

on the paste of Ponds' white on her face. Feels the cake of talcum
in her armpits. These revelations are becoming more difficult:
the clutter of potent seed spilling like this

to germinate in her fertile mind.
The dank smell of black earth and turning worms
drifts through the open window.

Clarice turns out the light and removes her robe.
In the half-light she catches glimpse of her profile,
the breast and nipples, the stomach's curve,

the vessel, so alive with its longings,
vacant like this for the rush of words to be carried
to the congregation. In the morning her dreams

will spill like confessions into the congregation's
upturned ear, distilled of the dross, the secrets of her tiny room,
while the believers garland her with her Sunday halo.

The bush at the bottom of the yard
rustles with the turmoil of midnight cats
and the screaming ejaculations of their sex.

The prophetess sleeps with her window open.
There is a moon uncertain of its light.
The wind stirs her curtains. She turns.

The moon catches the pink part of her lips.
On her bedpost perches the spirit – no ghost –
with a satchel of words for the congregation.

He feeds her in tiny morsels of potage,
gently wiping the overflow from her glowing chin.
She smacks her lips, then swallows. Turns.

CHAPTER III

Who Will Mourn for Her? (Nahum 3:7)

i

This Nineveh, tucked from the hurricane's blast,
riding the harmattan and lapped by the Atlantic turned foul
with the restless spirits of abandoned slaves

whose fish-gnawed bones never drifted to the broken
coastline of the rocky eastern cliffs facing Africa
all along the archipelago; this Nineveh city,

guarded by the wall of first defence and the decoy
of Cuba's agnostic bravado, is content and safe
in the warm thighs of the bearded Blue Mountains,

thumping with the wave-rock of the dip and sweet fall-back of
dancehall and gravel-voiced djs proclaiming
the new sound, the new prophecy of slackness.

The men feel for their airy crotches on the corner,
crawling from door to door discarding their progeny.
The women grind on the rain-slick street corners,

batty-riders wilding it up in the lewd light,
or lean their overflowing bosoms over the balconied
mansions of Beverly Hills, contemplating the new hunger

with its pragmatics of finding the right price every time.
Infidels skank to the visionless platform
of sweet-mouthed politricksters looking a contract

for their twilight years on the stump, rubbing 'risto shoulders
with the muck and blood of the ghetto – this
is retirement time, and every Christ is fixing

a tidy nest up in the sky for the greying times.
As the salt sea breeze catches the scent of the hull –
the rusty manacles, old red iron, the indelicate

farts of the souring bellies – head up always,
the worms crawl from their hovels at night,
watching for the quick stealth-dive of the gull.

They, insomniac in this new evolution of nature,
eyes bright infra-red darts, find the soft heads
and, quick bobbing, beak the crawlers.

ii

In this Ninevite valley, where the crossroads are sentried
with hustling preachermen among the broken
forms of slow-breathing madmen, who chuckle at the spectacle

in their all-black clothes shining to ciré in the sun,
the gospel is a three-card monte, crown and anchor board,
and the preacherman's hype is rapid fire and sweat.

Amazed and exhorted, the haremed sisters spur him on,
banging their arc of tambourines for the sinners
to come home, come home, come home.

The mawga sermoniser is black like a shak-shak pod
and dry same way, his body trembling out hope
of the precious gifts of the Almighty: the visa for a soul.

The testimonies are of those who have left;
the letters, read with ceremony and solemn ritual,
betray the lingering envy for those who have gone before –

thank God for his mercy – in the excuses, the rationalising
of the mysterious ways of the Lord. A sybil mother testifies:
"Brothers and sisters, the Lord has kept me here

like Paul, for he knows there are souls like you
to be won – for I woulda be walking the streets of Baltimore
with a green card and a Bible long time, but who

was going to sing this gospel unto yuh wutliss souls?
Is not one somebody me pray over an anoint with the oil
of joy for mourning right out there so on Oxford Street,

an is not accident mek the doberman guard
smile him bruk teet an seh, 'I see the glory. Hallelujah...'
An is not one somebody me pray up dem stairs

t'rough the raw smell and stink a dem ole neaga a try
defy the way of the Lawd fe de visa – People,
when time neaga a fret is a foul smell dem give off.

Me see one entry, multiple five-year visa,
me see multiple indefinite an even a green card,
an is not no saint dem, none a dem do de preachin what

this dawta of Zion do every blessed Sunday,
but dat is de way of the Lawd, and why a woman mus
bitter? De Lawd is good and fait'ful. Is me carry dem

a airport, me pay de taxi fare, me. For me not red-eye,
for I count it all joy whatever arrows the Lord
sen my way, for him nah go give me more dan what

I can bear. Amen? Amen? Amen! Amen!"
Tongues like fire in the place, and the sister holding
back the tears fire in her eyeball, heavy in her chest,

for this chastisement is hotter than anything she has known,
working down on her: varicose veins and the gas in her stomach,
the black swelling of her knuckles and knees.

iii

The poison of heaven's sudden curse
blows from Newark's phallic white towers,
spewing their toxic sperm into the fertile sky,

seeding her perpetually. She can't get enough,
they've been saying, she just lies there and takes it all,
then she lifts her skirts and blows south for the sun

across the Bahamas sky, too high for Haiti to see,
and then over Jamaica she aborts again.
Her rain of gaudy wetness jewels the beaches,

and the natives cough up blood and yellow phlegm,
balancing deftly the tropical rum punches on trays
through the sheets of tanning flesh on Morgan's deck.

In the shadow of an abandoned storefront
on Harbour Street, a squatting madman
shits his last meal with heartfelt reluctance

before the patient mongrel who has been
following for days for this repast.
This is the Ninevite valley

where on the hills the proffered open palms
of white satellites catch the passing rays
beaming-in a diet of soaps and family-value sitcoms.

Soon they are welcoming the swooping helicopters
with their marines and prospectors
with a satchel of visas, a constitution, a capitol hill.

"We will fly Dixie high if it's all we have to pay;
allegiance is a marketable commodity to us
ultimate merchants; we learnt a lot on the auction block.

Note the stump; our feet are impressed in it still.
We fit snug into the old mould, now new world order."

Seen from the bearded Blue Mountains

the valley shimmers like a bed of gems,
and the feet of the descending prophet, dusty with travelling,
hesitate as the air changes. The mint and pine

of the upper slopes are steaming into the humidity
of the million pyres glowing in the yards.
The feet shift, then stop.

CHAPTER IV

This Day of Aborted Beginnings

i

On a rain-drenched Sunday – no cricket. The sky
is heavy from the night before and the wind
carries ragamuffin sounds across

the Mona valley, dollying through
the craggy bramble clutching the tennis courts,
the almond-strewn swimming pool

mildewed with stale chlorine
and the stirred dust of a worn
but functional cricket pitch.

In the empty pavilion, Last Night gulps the last
of the sweet pippy wash, and spits out lime seed
arcing in the grey of the sky. The ragamuffin

changes with the wind. A new music rides the air:
the clapping of the congregation
from the Guild Building on the hill.

Last Night, belly full of clawing cheese
on hardo bread, lingers in the shed for fear
of returning home to Thelma,

her stabbing tongue and callous
taunts of the numerous hoods swallowed
by her well-deep public manhole.

ii

Last Night awaits the coming of night
when he will slip into his hovel
and plan his escape from the bitch.

Looking like poor t'ing on this day of aborted
beginnings, Last Night drips on the tiles
of the church hall as Clarice, on a roll,

points her tender finger at his forehead
and speaks his mind: "How far you think
you can run from the Lord? London,

Panama, New York, Columbia; even Havana
is part of His reckoning. How far you feel
you can run?" He is thinking

that it is not the Lord behind him but the bitch,
and this drama of his entry a chance
need for shelter and the sound of humans.

"And though you feel is the woman
you fleeing from, is the Lord behind you."
Last Night believes in that moment.

The Church gives praise to the prophetess
as Last Night tips
and kisses the tile, and tears

mingle with the rainwater.
Slain like this by the prophecy,
the intent of his soul is bared:

the flight to some injured coast
where another woman can
fulfil his multiplication of self,

this compelling logic of survival.
Why else the creation?
Why else the seed and fertile egg?

All is seen by the prophetess
who rests her sweaty thighs
on the metal seat and tries to sigh

the paddling sexy five o boys
from this holy moment,
seeing before her the fallen manchild

who has come here in this time of
weakness. Her caged mind,
cracking on the quiet, trembles.

Last Night gives his soul
to the Lord, and the congregation
sings, rejoicing at the miracle.

Through the raised hands
Last Night searches for her eye.
Her womb leaps.

CHAPTER V

Sovereign City

i

This was where Thalbot could be found,
the madman, would-be U.S. secret agent,
with a cache of classified information

padlocked, yale-locked, combination-locked
by his cage of insanity: the drooling,
the traffic guidance in the busy intersections,

the tanning of all his body parts
with a tourist's ceremony of toning his skin
with gutter mud and motor oil,

exposing the branch of his circumcised penis
to the women too curious to look away, too shy to stare
on its ungodly size – "What a waste, what a waste!"

ii

Behind the cracking grey colonial fence
had stood the jaded pink mansion;
slates of black checkered the roof, sucking in wind,

and the sweetest mangoes had hung there rotting
then plopped fermenting into the havoc of bush below,
for the small boys dared not risk the hail of stone

from Thalbot's overseeing perch on the hill.
This was before the city decided against preserving this legacy
of the past; before the marches and demonstrations,

the community meetings about eyesores and art;
before the pleading with the grinning Thalbot by the good
citizens from the Neighbourhood Beautification Committee;

before the bespectacled, Jamaicanised white English dread
from the Institute, with his jeep of spades and brushes
came to unearth the bones of slaves and their cowries –

only to be repelled by hyena Thalbot, waving his machete
at the ducking heads of the archeological party;
before all else had failed short of the police doing

what they said they would do and shoot the focking mad man
in the head; before the bulldozer ignored the gate
and took the grey wall out, then ploughed

its way into the heart of the estate, followed hard
by the insect-like mechanical spade, its pincers nodding sinister,
all come to grind the walls to dust. Then Thalbot had

awakened, ready for battle, black skin glowing,
like a maroon on a raid into a redcoat camp
with his machete slick and sticky

with the crystallising syrup of cane juice, and the mad
buzz of bees like a garland or talisman around his head.
Thalbot had resisted for three solid days, the drivers

fleeing, laughing but scared shitless, into the crowd
on Hope Road arguing about the wickedness of it all.
Then on the fourth day at three o'clock in the morning,

while Thalbot slept off a gift of potent weed,
they exploded the mansion, the walls crumbling
in sudden clouds of dust. Thalbot, wobbling,

startled by the cracking of the pine boards,
the shatter of glass where the wheels
crunched them into silica dust, could only stand impotent,

amazed at this quick demolition of his shelter.
Too late to fight, too stoned to shout, Thalbot had dreamed it all.
The pink sky of coming dawn had tinted this monumental task:

the broken tree limbs, the mounds of cement and brick,
the upturned soil, the scurrying cockroaches and rats,
the way the wind rushed in like the suck of air

into the space left by a pulled tooth, the tongue
probing, feeling the smooth hollow, still searching for
the comfort of that uprooted molar. The hole is deep and salty.

iii

He cannot be blamed for his instinctive return
to the place of his navel string's burial,
to the new monolith on Hope Road across

from the Liguanea Post Office where the
lignum vitae weeps its tears of yellow
and blue on April mornings, where *Malcolm X*

is showing and the children in their
nike and kinky hair are paying
good dollars for pop corn and drinks

chilling in the air conditioner's
bubble-gum scented air.
Sovereign City, market of foreign wares,

short only of the stars and stripes
and the bloated Elvis impersonator: Sovereign?
Now Thalbot must sneak in this glass and cement monstrosity

that covers the green and wild of his former glory
while the guardy and leashed bitch
steal a leak in the mint and jasmine public toilets

or go wandering after the riding ass of some
flaunting schoolchild traipsing through the artificial ferns,
slowly licking her million dollar ice cream cone.

At home again, Thalbot, the would-be secret agent,
returns to his sermon against the canker of colonial edifices
and impresses the gathering with his startling logic.

"As long as they break down that slavemaster castle
where a wild mad black man, naked as any Kojo,
been shitting and pissing and coming each morning

to desecrate the legacy of the whip and the chains,
as long as them wipe away the remembrance
of this artifact of the past instead of defecating on

its rass right there, so that our children won't forget,
then is this kind of shithouse imperialist
bloodsucking monstrosity going to rise from the ashes.

Me, Thalbot, was given the task to spray my poison piss
on the foundation of that Great House, to hold it
down until the wild Africa bush and vine

capture it around the neck and strangle it down,
down into the earth, into the soil where the bones
of the old slave people will do their work.

But see how the foundation catch a new wind and blossom
into this new babylon mansion. O Nineveh!
O Nineveh, how easy you forget the flame and whiplash.

Which part is the monument to the generations,
the evidence of the hoisting of the new flag?
In this shrine of jaundiced opulence?

In this temple to the gospel
of the dollar? This anointed structure prayed over
by the fundamentalist preacherman with him American twang;

Southern palmetto palms scattered through the island theme?
And the music, hear the music! Them put Marley
in a can and water him down to muzac!"

Entertained and amused, they giggle at his swinging dick
till the guardy remembers his calling
and wrestles the madman from the building,

blackening the walls and his toy-general outfit.
The smell of Thalbot's earth lingers for days
in the pure air of the glass-bubble mall.

iv

The prophet now plies his trade
in the traffic of Matilda's corner,
tempting the drivers to commit

euthanasia. Into the breach,
the hole left by Jesus, nailed hard
to the cross and then transported, enters

yet another voice, wailing in the wilderness.
This island spawns its prophets in plenty,
their ministry brilliant in the squalor.

Haven't you seen Don D or the Yout'
emerging yet again from the asphalt
with their magic teeth and split lips?

The people await the Coming
like shepherds in the field, curious
to see what two-headed monstrosity

will plop out this time into the bedpan
with cauls on his heads and songs
of redemption on his lips, what new path

to follow – though some Jobs and Nahums arrive unnoticed,
for the market is glutted with sybils and clarices
cornering the ready congregation with miracles.

So, numb like this, the city is deaf to the curve of their words;
just the spectacle of verbal acrobatics and scandal.
This is the Nineveh where Thalbot preaches his gospel.

CHAPTER VI

Denial

i

Deny it as she may, as she does,
denial three times over, denied
her nose, a fist of fired black clay

on her round bones and gummy flesh,
the heavy eyelids, now wrinkling,
the peppered coil of her hair, ropes

hanging in plaits over her broad brow,
this woman is black as burnt mahogany.
Africa clogs thick in her tongue

now twisting around King James' syntax
with her own stress and relax;
but her bleeding Christ has crystal blue eyes,

(to suggest otherwise would be sacrilege)
and her water-walker is clad in whiter-than-snow
seamless expensive threads,

(don't ask her not to covet the good things
in life, or not claim her bounty
as any child of a king should).

This sybil, in her white frilled blouse
stretched taut over the coarse starch
of her boned brassiere, she denies

her lips, her rocking waistline,
the way it lifts and turns, all buttocks,
balancing her sway to the bass-line

of the huge tambourine she batters
her yellow calloused palms'
rapid rhythm, and the brilliant light

of the tiny cymbals dancing in her head,
as the congregation bursts, all reverie,
all spastic shudder to the entering spirit.

Denying still the Africa of this meeting,
exorcising the suggestion of the word,
she prays for the noble missionaries

who have left the security and nostalgia
of their snowed-in Minnesota ranch to risk
being stewed in groundnut paste.

But how can I watch my grandmother
transported like this into the congregation,
hymning her lament, and not see her ululating near the river

where the boys shed their circumcision blood;
not see her journey along the coast
caped in its red scarf of sunset bleeding

over the drag of pebble at the surf's retreat –
here in this Elmina suburb, overlooked by the castle
where the bones grope blindly for missing joints;

not see her deftly pounding the pestle,
her green and black print cloth tucked high
up her tree-trunk thighs, thumbing the sweat

into the red dirt of this Akan coastal valley;
not see her leading the grandchildren through the bush
to the plot where she hoes the earth, turning over

the blanketed cassava among the scamper of
neurotic red ants? Deny as she may,
this sybil, corseted by her circumstance of birth,

she is still St. Thomas soil, black Maroon mother
with the curse of nigger in her rolling gait.
And though the fervid sermons have scrubbed

the moss from her skin, they have found
not pink, not whiter than snow,
but flesh red and tender as a wound.

ii

I will garland you in kente and bandana your
mystery head with the queen's cloth,
despite your protests and curses;

and in your dreams I will plant not
Toronto's blue sterility, where you will lie huddled,
old black woman coming to take another job,

and die with a visa and a social security card (for what?)
but the cool misty hills of Kilimanjaro's
piedmont greenery, where your yam will

twine about bamboo supports, and the nights
will gather in falling clouds across the
purpling skyline. In this dream, the youth

will journey the thirty miles on foot
to the kraal where you will anoint their heads
and speak your whispered conferences

with the one who comes from the lofty rock face
with a satchel of eternal truths ribboned
in cryptic proverbs and antiphonal song.

For though our heaven may be all nostalgia and created myth
it is my gift to you, sybil, while you sleep
to the symphony of gunshots in the tenement.

CHAPTER VII

The Old Man

i

In her powder-pink room at ten o'clock
Clarice entertains Last Night with bible verses
and prayers, casual in her yellow nightdress.

He has heard the shower, but dares not think
of the water beating her exposed skin,
her private stepping out of her damp panties;

instead he repeats the verses like a rosary,
his hands keeping down the fluttering jaundiced
pages of her worn bible on the dresser.

She returns still wet with yet another prophecy
about his lust for women, sexual disease:
the history of his secret encounters with whores,

and she spares no details for she has seen it all.
Taken thus by the memory, Last Night
tries to cover the discomfort in his groin,

but she has seen it and orders him to leave,
reprimanding him at the door
for his evil ways. She promises to pray.

Still he sees the flick of her hem
as she turns into the room, the way the flesh
of her thigh catches the light,

the gathering of her open robe, first straightening
the shoulder and exposing more flesh,
then clamping it shut, obscuring the powdered cleft.

Blue-balled and sick with his failings,
Last Night walks to his hole in the east,
now empty of the woman and her white rum.

He repeats the verses again and again.
Come Sunday, Clarice smiles that inviting way
and gathers the brothers to lay their hands

on his head, to cool the burning of his flesh:
the old man still wrestling, still rearing its ugly
pate, now to be buried once and for all at the river.

Last Night weeps his easy tears
with her sweat-soft hand resting
on his crinkled head, hot like that.

CHAPTER VIII

Changing the Guard

i

This nineteenth-century mansion reeks
of colonial decadence in the scent of stale
cedar and the chandelier's opaque crystals

dangling precariously from the cobwebbed
ceiling of the pine-wooded living room,
ribbed by the careful lines the light

draws through the lattice work. The glitter is gone;
the air vents are clogged with bat shit
and bones. On the living room wall an original

painting hangs, a roach-eaten water-
colour spotted white. In the half-light
the sunbathers are paler now, casual on the

Myrtle Bank pool deck, coconut trees waving,
a golfer poised over his putt, the wind
trundling the mountain of clouds above:

clichéd tropicana, and the natives, in tailored
blacks and stiff aprons, promenade with grins
like the griffins at the pool-head that spit

arcs of blue over the colonial postcard.

After the purchase and the signing of the deed
in the converted garage with its rats

and stale cheese and old rusty, impotent traps
among the oil cans and pools of caked
infertile soil, while the body still lies

warm in the white light of the cleanest bedroom,
the servants giggle over potent sorrel
and rummed-up Christmas pudding, preparing

for the ritual mourning to be held
beneath the bombay tree. Unemployed
now, they will miss fat Castleberry

and his gutted straw hat and cane.
The new tenants, a new age church
of middle-class believers, have decided

against helpers, gardeners and cooks,
and the smiling sly-eyed woman with her baggage,
the new caretaker, will talk to no one.

ii

At four o'clock, the family says farewell
to the now tipsy revellers, who still linger
before being ushered to their hovels,

complaining at the brusqueness of this new
woman with her familiar eye – they know too well
the way she understands their cutting eyes,

their slanting bodies; they understand her well-
cultivated snobbery; it is useless to resist it;
she is the new helper, gardener and cook;

she is the new presence of their shanty town,
the shacks and dust of Barbican's foothills,
where the slums are growing quickly: she has arrived.

In the vacant calm of their wake,
the setting sun sheds its red in patches
of triangular shapes on the stained tiles

of the porch, and the ghost sits transparent there
watching Clarice gather her breath at the
expanse of this front yard, her new domain.

Shrouded by the green of potted plants and vines,
and the blue curl of cigar smoke tickling the red ants
into vulnerable open spaces, playing chess

with the shadow and light of the tiles,
the ghost enjoys a good Havana. They have
waited patiently, the family, for the lump to burst

or whatever cancers do to kill. He fell into a pot
of ferns. Now dead, the deed signed, done the sordid
business of planting his carcass in Dovecot's lonely slopes,

they catch the 9:30 to Toronto where supper waits.
The slush quickly swallows their remorse,
drawing the humid stench of Kingston

from their heads, leaving it all behind,
this legacy, their father who lasted too long.
Now untethered, they search for new anchors.

iii

For two weeks Clarice delays her occupation –
the exact count is nine days, but the pagan
in her decision remains unspoken –

and in that time the house is silent;
the outdoor bulbs die quietly
and the garden sprouts a jungle of weed.

Thalbot, the drifter, discovers this new temple,
and occupies the garage as a first step;
patient, he will wait for the doors

to collapse from age before entering the sanctum.
But in nine days they arrive in teams,
volunteer cleaning crews

from church bulletin time, who have prayers
like potions for every corner, every
struggling mango tree. Thalbot,

ingloriously evicted with his shit,
vigils on the sidewalk, his nakedness
a weapon. But when Clarice arrives

with her dulcimena and baskets,
and gives him the full of her eyes,
lingering without winking at his

crumbled phallus, she slowly,
with calculated scorn, fixes his eye
and guides him to his feet. This prophetess's

eye washes his nakedness with shame
and he knows she has sanctified the mansion;
new mistress, new bitch of a queen.

It is her laugh that drives him sane,
and now unguarded, vulnerable in the city's
twilight, Thalbot dares not look back.

iv

Castleberry observes the arrival of the queen
and readies himself for the indulgence
of her company. She speaks to him

on the first night, declaring that in the morning,
if he is still there when she gets up,
he will be soundly cast out.

She also calls him a filthy old fool
for peeping at her nakedness
while she sings hymns in the shower.

CHAPTER IX

Confessional

i

"My damning fantasy, what cling to my brain
like bloodstain, a follow me like a hungry mongrel,
can' shake it off, can' turn it back..."

Last Night begins, in the white kitchen.
Clarice, domestic confessor of the wayward,
cuts the heads of skellions with quick

taps of the blade on the formica counter.
"Is a bad drunken woman, one who can talk
nasty about what she want a man fe do her;

a black woman with bold bright eye
smelling a talcum and sweet perfume
with old carbolic in the mix somewhere,

Lord forgive me." Clarice scoops the chopped
vegetables in her shining hands, green and orange
with slick wet tomatoes, and spills them

into the exploding dutch-pot oil; the onions
brown their crisp sweet smell in the room;
the radio plays Maxi Priest.

"An she can dance the bogle, with her knees
supple as guava switch, an everything so tight
that her back just a sweat an shine,

an her waist is like a pivot, an her batty bang
out like a Somali baby belly, shining crescents
under her frayed denim shorts." Clarice's back's

to him, her sexless body in a cotton shift
motionless, her two dusty sandals shuffling.
"An she don't wait for me to say what I want,

for she tipsy and bold, an she just want an want,
she smile her red smile, dear God, an her bad eye
tumble down pon me, an take it like that.

An all de while is pure slackness from her mout
a slap me one side an the nex wid her stinking word
dem. Forgive me, saviour – ah can just smell

the sweat and wetness. Why it won' leave me, sister?
After all is not lickle pray ah pray, but she jus
a come back." The sharp pricks in his groin

torment. He can't stop now. "Tumble down
on me, like that. Is wine she been drinking,
an it sour in her mout, an she jus taking an

taking what she want, all she want, everything, her hip
jusa ride an a turn... God forgive me, but is the truth,
Sister Clarice... Is like a bad dream, Sister. Won'

lef me, the way she abuse me, the way she shame me,
the way she jus mash me up dereso till she get
what she want, till she bruk with a piece a shouting

like she vex wid me. Then she just lif up herself,
draw up her garments an step over me so.
Not even a tank yuh, piece a dog shit, nothing.

An me shame like a dog with me something still
a stan up same way, no release in sight. So
me abuse myself, Sister Clarice, for what a man mus do?"

Clarice turns from the saltfish fritters
and slaps him pepper and onion across the face.
Falling in shock against the fridge,

his eyes water, his teeth cut his cheek.
She marches away with dramatic hissing teeth,
the oil still popping in the dutch pot.

Yet, through the haze, to his shame, he imagines
her hips swaying with too much accent,
her tightly-girded loins trembling.

ii

The brothers knock his door at six
to find him sweating after the shame of his dream;
he smells Clarice in the room and trembles.

The brothers wait for him, shadows
in the morning light, and lead him through the dew
and mist to the waiting vehicles.

The ghetto is sleeping; dogs drag their
war-weary bones to some shelter
of cardboard and junk before the sun comes.

They climb into the clouds of the mountains;
the river is turbulent brown after the overflowing
from the rains of the night before.

There waits the congregation
beneath the ficus tree: the new converts in white
sheets like Klansmen in the bush.

In intense caucuses, they chastise his sin
of a foul mouth, and then cast out the lingering spirits,
the childhood deprivations, the shameful acts,

the perversions of his corrupt mind;
and he feels the violent escape of demons
through a tidy round hole in his skull.

They fly through the ficus berry leaves
and he screams at their going;
his body now deflated, void, vulnerable.

The tears tightening in his throat,
this flowing, like the absence of muscle-
control in his limbs, his bladder, his bowels,

this slaying of the old man, collapses him. Clarice it is who
forgives his misguided soul, who pronounces
the judgment of the elders herself:

that they must not meet in seclusion after
this cleansing. Then he is dipped into the brown
thunder of the river, his white sheet now stained,

his soul revived by the turning dove.
It is nine o'clock when the hawk screams
over the Blue Mountains and, with a hymn

on their lips, the church descends into
the valley of decay – this Nineveh of their undoing.
Traffic stutters in Papine Square.

Last Night trembles and
Clarice reaches and clasps
his chilled hands in hers.

CHAPTER X

Hermit

i

In the filthy caves of Warieka, not Arawak bones
not hieroglyphs on the wall, just the Eritrean warriors,
heads too large, facing the Italian cavalry:

the blood of the white dead on the grass
in fading red; the golden brass of the Emperor's
mounted army; horses breathing fire.

This apocalyptic vision's set among the bones
of slaughtered goats, discarded garments
and the stale smell of smoke and urine.

In the yard, a mist ascends from the chillum
bubbling, and Ras Pedro, now street derelict,
hermit, whose unshorn locks cake

for want of practising ritual ablutions,
sucks in his daily dreams and revelations,
looking like the prophets of old gone mad.

The posses in hiding (most-wanted fugitives)
package pieces of pork each Sunday for a joke
and send a red-haired nigger orphan to Pedro

and his cracked drum. The dread accepts
the degenerate flesh – only, he says, to protect
another from partaking of its poison: "I shall

burn it on this holy mountain, as a fragrant
offering to Satan!" He does not touch the bloodied
newspaper. "Res' it over yonder in my shrine

to the shitty of Nineveh." He points to his latrine
where the groan of sluggish blue flies emanates.
Then at night, when the trouble of rapid digital

bass-lines climbs the craggy marl path to his cave
of bamboo and cardboard, he swallows the abomination,
stewed in onions and wild herb for cleansing,

peppered out with the scotch bonnets growing
like red sentries around his encampment.
Belching, humble and penitent, he asks Jah

for mercy. The goats are all dead now, their horns
piled in the broken shack to be used for his
mounded grave – this according to his last will and

testament scrawled in thirty exercise books
and still growing. From the slopes of Warieka,
Pedro observes his vast domain – the circle of magic

lights, the stadium constructed by Babylon where
once he sheltered in its unused tunnels until
the Queen of whores came visiting, and the walls

were limed to glorious white, and the prophets
were slaughtered, exiled to the hills, or locked into
the bedlam of Bellevue's knocking fans.

Pedro's drums are cracked now; the skins
have been stewed in curry and boiled;
he has eaten his gospel of truth.

ii

Clarice, who was born with his seer's eye,
has flown over the foothills and planted her
feet of news on the old beaten yard where as child

she mustered the chickens and sacrificial goats;
and at night serviced Pedro's lust and dreams.
Drawing back the curtain she saw Lot drunk and naked,

his black snake nodding on his thigh.
Having seen, she was taken.
Pedro prophesied her name in '58:

Clarice with eyes that penetrate
the sinew and bone; Clarice, with her mother's
skin and cheekbones, whose nimble fingers

construct fantastic designs from tattered fabric;
Clarice, the weaver of his nets; Clarice, waiting
there in the doorway for the weary drag of his

proud fisherman's body up the hill,
with sprats and snapper in his crocus bag
and the smell of sea in his beard;

Clarice, who spoke in strange tongues without prompting
on a night of drumming and revelations,
while the teenage would-be superstars,

climbing up from Channel One Studios with their
makeshift box-guitars and their heads full of songs
and fire, came to chant grounations with Pedro the teacher.

(Those who made it mention him in nostalgia
in their interviews, like one who died young,
lamenting their lost days of purity and righteousness

while they ride, bellies full, through New York and
L.A., sucking caviar, champagne, and custom-built
spliffs. Pedro is legend. That is all. Not even a smalls of gratitude.)

Back then, Clarice, the daughter in her righteous skirt,
would cook ital for the congregation of stoned
reggae denizens, playing her mother who, now

Miami-based, constructs a new past
in Fort Lauderdale, a past which excludes Pedro
and his slant-eye daughter.

Clarice saw her period motherless
and buried her wound in crocus sheets
until the first moon had passed.

Now, after all these years of absence,
after the secret departure one schoolday morning,
after the visit to the Government Office to declare

herself delinquent and a whore, after all these years,
Clarice returns in flight, her tongue now trimmed
to King James' metaphors, and she plants

a blessed kiss on his head. With no remorse
she promises to bury him well when he is ready.
She avoids the salvation message; his future is written,

prophesied and lived already; this interim
is redundant; nothing new will come,
marking time like this on the cloud of weed.

She carries a balm for his head and ministers it,
coughing at the dry smell of old sweat and sensi.
Found there in his nakedness again, this time he is

as potent as a discarded branch gathering dust.
In the hills, the guns echo where the posses
practice dodging Babylon's slings and arrows.

Pedro dreams, daughterless like this,
the chasm too wide; another life caught in the
bramble, another life bleating for attention;

but he is too old to try for another slaughtering,
another bloodying of the holy altar.
Clarice sees him beat his broken drum

again in the interim, the brief hiatus before flight,
his feathers drooping, tattered at the ends,
some broken at the quill: his wings, his

dull filthy wings. She sees his eyes: cataracts
consuming the light, no revelations on the cornea,
no premonition of safe landing on the plains

of Kilimanjaro, no Nile silver and blue
to barge down crowned in righteous glory,
no fledgling princesses to caress his wrinkled back,

no stool in the kraal with the shape of his buttocks
imprinted in the seat, no elders to meet him,
just this blurred spread of orange lights:

Kingston, the black of the sea, and the night.
Clarice takes his wrinkled face in her hands
and daubs the tears and caked matter from his eyes,

then brushes the gravel off his lips
with her own; he is not dead yet
this her father, broken prophet.

iii

Clarice abandons this Hades,
this reaching for hope and not touching,
this her perpetual nightmare,

her reminder of where she has come from.
Waking in the silence of the Castleberry mansion
she bursts into tongues, praying, "Mercy, mercy!"

CHAPTER XI

Infidelity

i

Last Night in overalls and dust mask
watches the dancing particles floating
in the stream of light, pinpoint laser

through the coke-bottle-green basement
windows, where the Africa collection
is stored in crates and mothballs.

He dusts and tags the pregnant Masai,
her ebony ears like swollen tears,
her skirt, the cured chipped bark of the tree,

clothing the spirit contained here;
her nipples, finely crafted, standing
erect as a preteen's fledgling berries.

Her head is shaped like the dome of an ant,
featureless, without lips, cheeks, nose;
the circular glow of light on the top

is her cyclops eye, following him. Last Night
labels the beads, the masks, the Ashanti swords,
the sandals, the stools – transported exotica

deposited in the Government's care by returning
Baptist missionaries, bearing these artifacts
like evidence of their travail with the heathen –

leopard skins now rotting in the dank hole,
ivory talismans, ebony paperweights,
some obi's cherished protection.

Overseeing this cache of culture is the tall
African-nosed black Baptist preacher, photographed
with his long coat and dangling gold chain

and his transparent wife, in white and frills,
framed there at the docks, in front of the crates
and the looming black of the schooner.

It has been sixty years since their celebrated
arrival, captured in the *Gleaner* as a native son
turned good, but the relics, once spectacles,

now gather dust in the basement. Last Night
executes his simple task without much regard
for the disturbance of the spirits, long trapped

in these nailed, cheap wood boxes, this vault,
still disoriented by the long sea passage, blown by
the harmattan of Sahara's season of dispersal.

But the Masai woman draws him in
with her cyclops eye reflecting his sweating face,
and with soft strokes of the chamois cloth

he tickles her offered breasts,
feels for the kick of infant long carried
in her jutting navelled stomach;

and without understanding the heat
in his armpit, he removes the dust mask
and places his lips on her smooth forehead.

Transported for an instant to the outskirts of her village,
he sees her neck like a giraffe above a thorny hedge
as she herds the cows, her teeth chewing grass.

He peels the bark of old wood from her waist
and stares at the smooth ebony of her thighs;
then, praying like mad, he falls.

ii

When Clarice reads his mind –
like spinning leaves in the teacup bottom –
and starts with a scream of recognition,

when she asks what light he has looked into,
what pot dipped his fingers in,
what whore he has paid for flesh,

Last Night is speechless and confused.
"Yuh been eyesing the nakedness, eh?"
Clarice's prophecy, like a wife's accusation

sanctified by a sudden hallelujah,
startles his heart. "That will be
your downfall. You don' see? Them waiting,

always waiting for some fool-fool soul,
clean and sweep with a good broom,
to come seckle dem conniving ways in."

"It was jus' a statue…" he starts. "A simple
statue. And after all, what a man must do?
This game yuh playing turning me fool."

But she has stopped listening and turns away,
blows by him, carbolic and sweat-tinged perfume;
then she is swallowed into the pink and yellow of her

forbidden room, but leaves the door ajar
like parted thighs, hinting at the bright
and wet light of her beckoning.

The priestess waits for his arrival in her temple
with her satchel of penance and her chastisement.
Last Night hesitates at the threshold, sweating.

CHAPTER XII

The Fear of Prophecy

What else has she seen during Sunday's
sluggish worship time? I think of the morning
after the thing with the mango and Jennifer,

proffered like Eden's infamous fig,
and the maddening scent of sex in the moustache
after the flight like Joseph leaving his

manhood and dignity in Potiphar's wife's
welcoming bed. That Sunday I sat in the cacophony
of tongues and souls reaching upward,

that sometimes touch with a shudder and amen,
and tried to force a purer image into my mind,
as if Clarice's prophecy required my writing

a digression of bright images in my brain,
trying like hell to push away the image of Jennifer's
knees knocking on my ears, and her voice saying,

"This is what I have longed for, longed for."
Then electing to keep the eyes open,
(for closed, they return to Potiphar's chamber)

I seek out Clarice's eye, as if to psyche her out,
and this is all I do through the whole service,
my heart throbbing, my stomach churning.

But Clarice sits in her seat of power, eyes closed,
smile beaming in some transported reverie.
Is it me she is reading, falling again, is it my

fantasy, flaming with its startling detail?
How fully I repent, how deep my weeping,
my lamenting before the altar.

So afterwards, I greet her with a kiss
of gratitude, for she should know
without my speaking that I am grateful

that she did not do her bounden duty
and point her finger in my open face
and shame me before God and the brethren.

CHAPTER XIII

Sunday Morning

Bougainvillaea spills its tongues of yellow
and specked blood on the outdoor ballroom
floor and the steel drums rust in the puddles

from August rains. Here, on the aqua tiles,
now fading, the water pools in the sinking foundations;
the dry upper ground is strewn with

goat shit where the goats shelter from the deluge;
bramble lies scattered like debris of sea-
carved wood on a fresh Friday beach.

Here, with the six o'clock morning cloud cover,
the cool breeze licks the shak-shak pods.
Prayers turn heavenward. In the makeshift

chapel-sometimes-gymnasium (where on weekdays
sweating first-years play;
their symphony of ping-pong

dropping like rain: soft sponge,
plastic on wood, their soles squeaking
on the slick floors), the folding

glass windows are stained. The janitor
says the water seeps into the double plate
and stays preserved like that for years. In the yard

behind the building, strewn with bloated plastic
chemical bottles, old film, and the stench of sulphur,
cows graze in the gungu vines and mud,

penned in by the stripped coconut stems and bamboo
strangled by plaits of barbed wire. The soil
is always soft; clay is splattered on the walls

beneath the dripping air conditioner, jutting its
rusting mechanics into the elements. Through
the glass, the avenue of pines sheds

its yellow cones; coolie-plum trees drop
a squishy pungent carpet of fermenting yellow fruit
and dizzy bees. The crooked trees, like starved

acolytes, reach for the praise of song and raised hand.
The campus is overrun by butterflies on Sunday mornings
and, as the sermon flames its tongue of deliverance

in the fanning flurry of the congregation for Christ,
this is the distraction that swallows my wandering eye.
Dreaming is easy in this dream window

landscape and, if I stare long enough,
(pushing back the tambourines and tongues, the muttering
and grunts of possession and release)

at the play of green, yellow and ochre of the wild gungu
vines, I sometimes come away, like David from the wilderness
of olives and eucalyptus green, glowing for my indulgence.

This romantic interim in the passion of gospel reverie
is sometimes all there is to keep you rooted there
in the clamour of your sins, your falling, your remorse.

On Sundays, sometimes, they think I have died inside,
unfeeling to the prophecy coming like the wind,
the bright red blood of Christ in the crystal decanter,

when my eyes dance the leap and dip of yellow butterflies
turning around the cakes of green, fresh, fly-thick
cow shit. The sky winks through the leaves,

and in the precious glass-bowl silence, caught in my
own life-giving bubble of indulgence, the voice carries
clear over water. I am saved again without a shot being fired.

PART TWO

When an evil spirit comes out of a man, it goes
through arid places seeking rest and does not find it.
Then it says, "I will return to the house I left."
When it arrives, it finds the house unoccupied,
swept clean and put in order.

Matthew 12: 43

CHAPTER XIV

The Making of a Prophet

i

In Parade, the lignum vitae sheds its leaves,
strangled at the roots by the pink cement
of a gaudy beautification programme

where the grass has been transported
from some nursery in Hope Gardens
and dared to sprout and thrive

in the smoke and din of Parade Square.
The madmen have marked their spots
in balding patches along the lawns.

The old dowager queen looks down
upon the squalid populace, her
cheeks sagging Gillespie-like.

The bird shit is like stone
on her head now. Nobody cleans her
but the rain. Even the birds have stopped coming.

And Marcus walks unnoticed in the crowd,
book in hand, without words, without a congregation,
going nowhere in his good suit and tie.

ii

Three whores, modestly drawing down their hems
over the cheeks of their meaty bottoms,
commandeer a taxi to journey

to where the clubs are emptying
and men are looking a warm front for the night.
The taxi man is nervous. His squawking radio,

with its gutted viscera of yellow, red and blue
spilling onto the weather-rusted floor
of the cab, announces murders on the hour,

and the whores smell sharp, hard as nails in the back.
A gravel-voiced one asks the cabbie,
her legs spread wide in the rearview mirror,

"Who fa pum-pum this is, Cabbie? You know?
Yuh can pay fa?" And empowered like this
the whores laugh, slapping old Cabbie

in his ailing head. He bows and keeps on going.
Cabbie undercharges and unloads them with their rockus
laughter into the orange glow of Knutsford

Boulevard where they parade their sex
in the shadowed doorways of foreign embassies.
They service the new club scene in Kingston

where the Shabbas, Supercats, and the gaunt
malnourished Cool Rulers make a living
reheating leftover hits for the city elite.

This is the watering centre of Kingston's payola district,
where the politicians all talk of the shared ideologies
in this basin. Long gone is the socialist puritanism, gone

the old revolutionaries who have
discarded their bush jackets, (hand-me-downs to
gardeners) who now concede without fanfare to

the pragmatic wisdom of the IMF.
With vanishing hairlines, grey wrinkled heads
and eyes that seem to strain in the glare of flashes,

they read softly from the teleprompter like geriatric pimps:
"Come to Jamaica, come to our wonderful
island paradise, where the whores are

spicy as jerk pork and the reggae shrines
await your US green. Come, come, you can buy
a piece of Marley here, get stoned on his

grey tombstone. Come to Jamaica and *I* will
feel alright." Boom times in Kingston and the cocaine
floats with its dust of sudden dreams. Restoration Kingston.

These are good days, cash times for the whores,
some making hard dollars with malleable waistlines
on the dancehall videos clotting the airwaves.

This is the shocking-out of the sisters,
their sexuality like a fresh new banner
sold to the highest bidder, and the boops weep.

"For is dis de woman dem want!"
the smirking, beleaguered gold-chained dj protests.
"For is pum-pum rule the world now, and

the daughter dem a flex out, flex out."
The charts are exploding, the money is coming
and dancehall gone Grammy and all. And in

an executive suite of New Kingston Hotel a woman
spreads on silk sheets and smiles:
"Who fa pum-pum this, Yankee. Yuh like?"

iii

Two angels with briefcases
and diplomatic immunity
landed in Kingston from heaven

on American Airlines
to investigate a huge problem.
You see, heaven had been infiltrated

by this new thing called posses,
and what with the Mixicans
sneaking in through the back door,

the Haitians avoiding Peter's scrutiny
and clogging up Purgatory
(which was meant for white folks

from Europe who were being
punished for their faithlessness),
and what with the complexity

of the new dispensation,
with Satan now a friend
and hell not as exotic as it used to be,

why, heaven was in complete disarray.
And now these posses with their
peculiar, Satan-inspired plots

had infiltrated heaven
and the angels were getting vex
and wearing back their white robes and thing.

So, the two crew-cut
special agent from heaven
choose to come incognito,

so them forego the Jacob ladder
business which would cause
too much attention.

Now this was not an invasion
or anything like that. This was simply
to solve one serious case.

Pseudo-dread Thalbot
was the target. See, Thalbot
have some details about one of the posse

and the plan was to carry Thalbot to heaven
to finger the impostor, in exchange for
residence, much milk, and honey.

Now Thalbot had always been
a hospitable man, and he fed them
rice and peas and let the angels

lust a little after his daughters,
for what harm could there be
in a simple thing like that?

And truth be told, when Thalbot
heard the deal, he know he couldn't
pass it up, for part of the message

was a simple one: Jamaica, being so
close to this satellite of hell, could
get a touch of the smart attack

when it came to Cuba – and it was coming
like the rapture – so who could blame
Thalbot with his two daughters,

who already feel like heaven is
the only place could save their wayward
self from sodomy and AIDS.

But word carry fast in this city
and a bunch of serious fellows
gather like military front of Thalbot house

demanding to see the angels them.
Now "see" is not a easy word,
for if you hear them talking, you would know

that "seeing" business would involve
some pain. Well, most people would
wonder why such deviltry consume the people,

but you tell me, you know anyone
would grudge them guys from sodomise
the two angel, after so much shame and disgrace

begging for visa, day-in, day-out, only
to have them turn you back again and again?
You tell me somebody who never even

think bout take one of them dead-face
visa official and sodomise them little rarse
right there and then. Like is something you begging?

Now, nobody could say Thalbot never try.
The man send out his own girls,
but you know the story, right?

Well, them angels come prepared
and one wave of the hand and every
single man out there gone blind,

so that the people them could leave
in the big white Cadillac and ride
to Palisadoes for the next flight to heaven,

visaless,
passportless,
but diplomatic in style.

iv

They travelled quickly through the dead streets,
heading past the Rockfort cliffs, broken
by dynamite, bright in the silver moonglow,

to Palisadoes where the round-tipped, slick cylinders
of planes land nose first with a hint of rainwater
from the clouds to make entry smoother; Palisadoes

where the coconut trees part like damp pubic hairs
and the planes land swift and soft
on the shimmering tarmac, guided by lights

in the salt air. This is where the convoy of Thalbot
and his daughters was headed. The wife stayed behind
with her longtime lover, to come later, she said.

But Thalbot, staring at the fading mountains behind,
with the thought of the boredom of heaven
turning over in his head, hesitated. The taste of

jerk pork, some hot pepper and a warm Red Stripe
became a craving, an impossible need. He stopped
the car, for a second, he said, at the circle of vendors.

The angels were reluctant but waited while Thalbot
did his thing. When they looked away, he took off
sprinting into the maze of duplex homes, into the hills.

His daughters were screaming for the new heaven
and the way it was changing to suit their tastes.
The angels were all forlorn and a little afraid.

It did not take them long, however, to decide
on a new plan. The daughters became the informants,
imbued now with power in their finger tips.

Briefed like this, they boarded the plane for heaven
and then, renamed with the careful skills of the
angels they relocated to Indiana and vanished.

V

Thalbot watched from the hill
as the plane slipped swishing over
the tarmac and bore into the clouds,

heading south to catch the wind, and then
swung north. Then he walked the path
to the burnt husk of his home,

his family now myth, his home, broken,
his feet growing weary of shoes
and his memory shot. Thalbot's spirit

took in the voices of ghosts
who roamed these streets
still smarting from their multiple wounds.

Obedient to his new calling, he listened
for the poems that came lifting through the arc of the sun,
passing the moon. Thalbot prophesied unto the stones,

and formless trees raised their hands and clapped;
the wind whispered as the ghosts walked again.
"I have heard them in the dead of night, coming."

This was before the destruction of his shrine
on Hope Road, before the eviction of his
stored memories from the vine shelter

by the pincered mechanical spade and bulldozer,
by government writ and neighbourhood paranoia;
before the shrapnel eye of Clarice

stripped him to shame on the skirt of the Castleberry
mansion; before the colour of tomorrow
grew so dim that prophecy seemed like a stone;

before the scrambling of his mind;
before his death-in-life in the whale's belly;
before the rain of fire on this Nineveh.

CHAPTER XV

Legion

A camera metaphor must be engaged
for this *mise en scene*. Pragmatic Judas
stands in the crystallised salt on the deck

there on the Galilee Sea and mutters,
"Is that not a patent waste of good
fresh pork? The Gentiles like it jerked

in pimento and ginger, soaked like that
for days with a touch of their brown
slave sugar. They pay good money for

this – and what of the poor hog farmer?
You see him leaping hallelujah on the
craggy stones, frightening the wild gulls?

I won't even mention the rights of the pigs."
To catch this kosher miracle,
this parable in sacrificial slaughter,

close in tight on a gnarled finger, (use a red
tint to avoid conferences, subcommittees,
Trent-like councils debating His complexion)

cut to the frothing chap – filth like a second
or third skin and a distinct madness in
his eyes. This you will see from the quick

zoom-in: red eyes darting. Forget sound;
the image will blow your mind with its own
music. Then the startled scream, no mouth,

no source, just this curling surround-
sound and hear the sharp intake of breath
in the zombied theatre. Pan now, pan

so fast the olive grove is a blur, the
ochre rocks a line of reddish yellow,
like streaks of bird shit across

a windshield with stupidly waving wipers,
and the plate sky seems still with the
sparrow dip-winged and darting with

the pan. (You may have to do
several takes to get this right.) The pigs
must look like hogs, swine even,

chomping some old carcass in the suddenly
bleak day, blood indeed, and slimy viscera
when the camera pan stops. Then, as if startled

by this glare of the camera,
(which, you well understand now, contains
the legion of stirred-up demons who

scream like kids on a roller coaster ride,
wild expletives mingled with laughter and
the subtle smell of loose shit) the swine will run! In their mud

and blooded jowls, the swine will stump and
stumble, as the camera, handheld and
unstable, follows the piggish stampede,

wild screaming stirred by a few choice
off-camera blows (the disclaimer in the credits
will silence the SPCA), and tumble, tumble,

keep that pan moving until the cliff
edge where a stampede camera
catches the flap of teats and hog balls

leaping into the churning sea. Ahhh!...
This miracle is only complete when
the cut-away returns to the man

now robed in symbolic white, his hair
a tad cleaner (they expect this – bluff it)
and Christ grinning. "Whose blasted swine

were those? Ever thought of what
all that rotting pork and chemical run-off
could do to the fragile ecosystem?"

This is an optional voice-over
for the cynics. Otherwise wash it with the strings
you always wanted to use. This is

a demonstration of the drama's importance
in these things. The converts will come, seen
this way. It is not extraordinary.

We see it again and again. The wind picks
up on the sea and the waves lurch
steep and high. The man is taking off

His sandals. He does not mind
His feet getting wet a bit. Do not try
to add this to the film, miracles are hard to fudge.

Trick photography appears cheap and tacky
and the mystery is the thing, after all.
But a solid parting shot is everything:

Picture in medium frame, but colour sharp,
the ex-insane arguing animatedly
with the swine herdsman about the hogs;

then a long shot with the tip of the ship's bow
cutting into the chop of the sea, with Christ,
arms open against the tumbling storm,

white robes flapping in the wind,
his hair like gold ribbons in the greying sky;
then the chopper shot: the swooping eye

of the steady-cam panning the wrinkled sea surface.
Then, pulling back, see mountains and blue sea,
and the boat bobbing in miraculous light: sunset.

CHAPTER XVI

Communion

On first Sunday, with the grey metal
table covered in flowing white, the
decanter catching the light, red with

Wincarnis, and those loaves of hardo,
Christ's body before the miracle,
from the country church come visitors,

three kings and two queens, the kings glowing
in their pink and blue gabardine suits,
the queens all in white, beating their tambourines,

their antiphonal shouts stirring the congregation,
though some will not move for fear
their hips will lose decorum.

On first Sunday, the cup of salvation
bearing His blood is passed
from lip to lip in heavy tumblers,

while the congregation sings,
"The blood that gives me strength..."
Clarice smiles her benign way

on the grateful who have seen
her clairvoyance, this fantastic magic
that has not come from the delicate

pastries of the loafer and chalice,
but from the yam mounds, the
Warieka marl pits, the lignum vitae's

subtle voice, the jasmine, the cedar,
the mahoe. Clarice speaks from
the covered table, her bible with

its supple broken neck, wind
fluttering the pages, the power of the word
now cutting through bone, marrow,

the word resurrecting Lazarus,
the stone moving. The sisters
shudder and shout, while the brothers

groan to the belly-roll they feel.
It is coming, this wind and fire.
But here in the interim, in this lull

between the spoken word and incarnation,
the explosion of new mornings, enters
Thalbot, drifting like wind-borne newspaper.

There is no alarm on his arrival,
but the presence jerks up the heads,
and Clarice turns to this walking prophecy.

A tambourine tinkles. A baby screams.
Clarice points her finger to the dizzy
crows who dive nose first

into the Liguanea Plains, navigating
with their frantic tails the sharp,
sudden descent. Thalbot falls.

Clarice prophesies into his panting body.
The sisters gather and clean Thalbot's
body of residual spirits, the froth

of spit from his mouth and the grime
on his face. They feed him bread
and wine while Clarice falls into

tongues and weeping. Clarice sees
again the rain of crows from the sky.
Someone testifies the same vision;

the congregation sighs.
Thalbot rises slowly. Miraculously
the songs flow familiar from his lips

and tears seep constant,
streaking his clean cheeks,
salting his broken mouth. Amen.

CHAPTER XVII

It is the Cause (Bellevue Ska)

"Love is Earth's mission
despite the massed dead" (McNeill)

i

The first visitation came riding the flapping
coat tails of a ska syncopations, and the
rudies with their dawtas in mini skirts

and helmet heads smelling of the singe of the iron,
chopped scissor-slashes between their legs,
bowed, bobbed, grinned through the sweat,

eyes blazing like midnight riders in the Glass
Bucket Wine and Dinery to the blast
of Django's gunfire first, then the trombone calling

back across the black sand of the southern coast,
Yallahs, where the slaves buried the laid-out
body of Queenie, now travelling the miles

to familiar soil, Takoradi, Lome, leaving behind
a dynasty of prophetesses, who now spray the rum
and shuffle in the dust yards around the pole.

The ghost with cauled eyes
and a green vision of Addis Ababa
lingering like sand in his soft eyelashes

is silent on the bandstand, watching
Africa in the dances of these partygoers,
here in Kingston's hip jazz clubs of the sixties.

He is eyeing like a dream the pelvic flirtations
of Anita, the rumba queen, whose hopes of
heaven in Batista's Cuba have blown up red

like revolution, and now she ekes a less glamorous
fame in the shabby ballrooms of the city,
waiting for New York to call, for Vegas, for Frisco Bay.

The horn man intoxicates his
vulnerable mind with her perfume.
"O prophet, how can you see through

this haze?" wails David over
the foetal remains of his misconceived
offspring, the ghost of the Hittite

walking the old balconies
where Bathsheba shed her skin
and threw fidelity to the wind.

And Joseph, sprinting in his technicolour
dreamcoat with a voice sweet as a choirboy,
gropes in the corner for his tampered testicles,

and, wincing at the high laughter of Potiphar's wife
watching his frisky righteous butt vanish
behind the arras, says: "Don't do it, don't do it!"

"Don't do it!" says Elijah beneath the naked tree
in the wake of his lust for Jezebel, whose flesh
nourishes the dogs that shit her out into the faecal rivers.

But Don, the horn man, pulling his bell,
finding the distempered melody
in his puffed cheeks, his tongue

toying with the brass, tonguing the
patois into the ride of the ska,
the ride of the new jazz from Alpha

to the Omega of Thalbot's fertile soul,
what does he care about the cuckolded Panamanian
boxer, Anita's old custodian and pimp,

in this fire of their silent lust
burning up the Glass Bucket's dance floor,
making the prophet fall like that?

And when the Cosmic journeys after
the falling of his mind in Bellevue's silent
dust, it is the murderer's gaze that leads,

as with fired missionary zeal, white shirt
tucked tidy, standing there with three
days' sweat and as many sleepless nights

in his eyes, he guides the traffic
in Cross Roads's crisscross of lanes with his finger,
a rotating compass making perfect circles.

In his head the blast of horns,
the impatient expletives are applause;
the rotten fruit, bouquets of roses.

Possessed like this, after near twenty years,
after the secret burial in the Catholic cemetery
with a weeping mother and priest and nun

who minister over this self-abused soul,
praying their penance for the last rites;
after the natty dreads recapture the tombstone

in Jah's name with rituals of incense and sensi;
after the cut of the kete in the midnight air;
after the gunshot and arrests; after all this,

the spirit of Don the horn man reinvents itself
in Thalbot, the prophet, who guides the Black Maria
to an empty alcove, and waits, arms outstretched, for the bangles.

ii

Waving away the cobwebs,
he follows the path into the gloomy
belly of the shuddering van,

and carried away like Bedward
to the fluid calmness of injections
the white walls and bed,

in his head the song again:
"You pray tonight, Anita?
It is the cause, it is the cause. Whore!"

iii

The boys sprint in the interim,
riding the smoky jolly buses,
chanting, chanting. The traffic renews

its own insanity, and a generation abandoned
by its prophets and dreamers
searches for its old vomit,

while the horn man, blinded,
sees the machete dripping blood.
Anita's wounds, like Caesar's,

sing their arias:
the accusers at last finding
voice on her porcelain belly.

CHAPTER XVIII

On the Road to Emmaus

i

The second apparition, or spirit (we have
yet to settle on the fitting noun for the haunting,
the possession after nine nights of rum),

arrives on a luxury liner that
rocks in mid ocean with the dizzy egrets,
bearing promise of land in their beaks.

His cancerous eye and muddy skin,
though familiar with the heat, don't take
to the sun too well. Notice the pale

of the belly and the inclination towards
cultured things like cafes and wine at meals
and the perpetual cigarette dangling like a murder

clue from his blackened lips. Sweet on Greek
classic structures and tragic consequence,
he sees Achilles, Christ and Jason in the Kingston slums.

In typical melodramatic fashion,
his calling was with a bolt
from the blue (in fact the sky was black that day

with the acrid smoke of riot and arson),
on the Road to the Central Police Station
in pursuit of a citizen's duty and a solid three o three

to quell the misguided uprising of the masses.
He did go blind for a minute and then, miraculously
healed, he chose the lazy path of literary schizophrenia.

His return is unheralded; no one sees him on the ship's
deck: these tourists are immune to the spirits.
Thalbot, there on the wharf, transacting

a smalls with an old school friend, is chosen for his
shabby garments and unkempt hair. The transformation
is momentous: the change in tastes, the passion

for cold duck and turkey, good American cigarettes
and cool neat cognac. He ducks into the Bamboo Lounge
to hear some jazz and take in some art, protesting

at his inexplicable eviction from the premises.
At last the sun seems welcome on his skin.
Nigger like this, he merges into the masses and sweats

their sweat, meets their eyes and, caged in his
armour of filth and blackness, lives his fantasy.
In Parade he stands akimbo and intones:

"O Kingston!" in the sweet round voice of a prophet,
so familiar now, so appropriate. "O city
of desolate lanes and multiple Christs,

charting new gospels in the dust, barefooted
and dignified as well-trained messiahs,
embrace me now, I have returned renewed!"

He discerns the rooting of memory
in the reggae thumping from the sound systems,
but how casual they all seem about this treasure

in their midst. "Prophesy!" he urges. "From the Bible.
Like the blind Tiresias, speak truth. Prophesy
to the swine and mongrels on the garbage heaps."

His novels sell well these days. Children
learn of the myth of his conversion in high school
and giggle at the quaintness of his fantasies in prose.

The women seem tougher and more intent these days;
they do not go mad in the streets
after gutting their wayward lovers. No, they

clean the knife of finger prints and wail murder
into the chaotic night, then in black they bury
and recover quickly. New day, new day.

The sun sets bloodier than he remembers.
He feels a poem swelling. Thalbot balks at the thought
of finding a pen to write it down. He will talk it.

But it comes out like sawdust in the new air,
this rhetoric of fire next time, this red revolution,
this talk of rising masses and swinging sickles.

The interim is too long. Who would have guessed
the Castros, the Gorbachevs, the Munroes now
turned to clichés? He has waited too long.

His spirit, discouraged, longs for the sea
where the fish play tunnel games with old bones,
now one with the coral and volcanic stone

cooled into fantastic colour by the rush
of water, carved into art, calmly becoming again
where the whole thing found first shape.

Away from this, stifled by the smell of mortality,
dizzied by stooping for long-discarded poems,
like a madman gathering scraps of glass and metal,

drawn by the salt air Thalbot falls like a tossed log
from the jetty on a purple green night
into the salt and suck of the ocean.

In the black water, the bite of sand
and the tickle of weeds on the naked feet,
drowning, drowning, they part ways.

Thalbot pops like a buoy to the surface,
breathing, breathing, and then, spent
and void on the black sand beach,

he languishes in the fishbones and guts
and cracked canoes left by the fishermen.
The spirit stays off the coast, eying the sun's

journey; it is too late for old prophecies.
The children plash in the morning, diving
for conch and black coral. The fires of

stirring fishermen's wives glimmer on the beach
among the twist and tangle of sea grape trees.
The spirit watches the seine's curve over the Caribbean
coming up empty.

Then down among the sunken ships
and peaceful ghosts of the sea-buried millions,
the spirit finds his resting place.

Thalbot, abandoned, is walking
the cragged south shore to Kingston;
the wind blows through his vacated carcass.

CHAPTER XIX

Equinox

i

The third apparition parted ways with his spirit
on the docks of Charleston in January
as the flotsam nudged the waterlogged jetty.

Drunk and dizzy like the winging
gulls, he stripped to his paler yellow
armour and then collapsed deflated on

his gabardine bush-jacket suit, the scars
where the knife had plunged, where the pistol
whipped his scalp, still tender

despite the years. The sailors
and whores gathered to see,
but none would touch this drunk red nigger,

left for dead though simply pissed,
his eyes rolled back. But embarrassed by
the shame of dying needlessly, and the signal

of chemicals rebelling in his brain,
his soul ejected and danced over
the harbour, shivering in Atlantic winds, going south.

His mind, said "Ward Twenty-One",
had unhinged with the disappointment
of multiple rejections. The Americans

had no time for this poor West Indian
who had spent his seed in coconut tree splendour
returning prodigal in this bitter winter

crying "Home! Home!"
It was not racist or anything so satisfying,
just the insignificance of his return.

So, rejected and jobless,
he returned to the stink and dust of Kingston,
the heat on the tarmac like a neckchoke.

The turning John crows saw the deadness
in his drooping head and shuffling gait;
even the beggars spared him from embarrassment.

Dispossessed, for the soul had taken flight,
his body slowed on the stroke side,
no more fire, now plump old-people's-home-

sweet, he patrols the city in a tattered hat,
its gaping holes exposing the softness of his skull
and a million words unwritten.

The soul, long returned to the Gordon Town
hills searching for a worthy body,
after aborted efforts with two fat cows

and a Papine goat, (all three now dead – so unused
they were to creativity) finds Thalbot available again.
In his head things begin to take shape:

the self-righteousness of his political angst,
the insufferable posturing of a young man's guilt
at his denials of the poor at the gate,

for what wronged helper now conquered by the worm
could hear or care to give a damn
or dram of forgiveness to the spit in the eye,

the mucus of rotting colonial castles?
It all seems useless now.
On a clear day, from the porch, when Kingston

is calmer and the ships prod at the coves, he recalls,
instead of politics and the masses, the buried pleasures,
the objects of his shame: Myrtle Bank and the balls,

the jaunts to Negril with food, two servants
and a driver like furniture;
cricket at Melbourne park, white on the green;

the tea, the rum, the sweet memory of summer skirts;
the BBC World News, *Caribbean Voices*;
pounds and pennies, rugby and Oxford;

trips on the boat to Paris, writing bad poems
of autumn leaves and sweet white girls who smile
at the uniform and the curl of cigarette smoke;

the whores, the crude gentility of cockney lovemaking –
forgetting the skin, the slight nigger shade
below the well-kept surface, the darkness after.

All these, like postcards with no text, are things longed for
after all these years of denying the pleasures
of the old colonial class: honour and order in the world.

ii

So when asked about Progress and Independence
by the young undergraduate trainee reporter
come to do a special feature before he dies,

he replies, "I miss those colonial days," and regrets
saying it, the way her eyes water and her head falls,
the way her ites, green and gold, seem like a reproach.

"It is not what you think," he wants to say.
"I have not sold out... it is age; you become
cynical and you sip your indulgence of vodka

daily for a jar to the mind. Of course,
you have heard Marley and seen the light
of this Africa revived, but it is not new.

Hell! I wrote of the slaves and drivers,
the archeology of our retentions. I have paid my dues.
I had a black lover too, my most honest love.

They beat me up for loving the people
and my books are taught in schools... I am
just so damned tired and all my friends are dead..."

But she has risen, gathered her papers
and slipped through the creaking gate, her
tape recorder and satchel of his yellowing texts

slapping against her thigh; she has not seen
the slight beckon of his raised hand, nor the wetness
in his bright eye. His mouth moves, talking to the wind.

iii

…We are burying our brains,
our Rhodes Scholars, our people of letters
and the tenured, nailed-down intellectuals;

but we fear the village is emptying
quickly, and the children, untethered, have
abandoned the kraal. They leave the frames

of the houses to sway in the dust,
and the words that remain in the trees
grow jaundiced with overuse.

CHAPTER XX

Requiem for the Harrowed Poet

i

Unhinged like this, the door flaps
in the easterlies, the scent of salt cod,
starfish and oil stirring the dry sea grape leaves.

This gaping doorway is the soundless mouth,
the eyes boarded up, not seeing, not seen,
and when the storm comes, the roof stays intact.

Inside there is the smell of old meat rotting in the
chemical stench of the hot refrigerator,
and here, like pestilence, the croaking lizards set up camp.

ii

He stands on Old Hope Road with his hands
outstretched as in prayer, and his penis,
nestled like a chunk of tractor tyre in the rope

and camouflage of his pubic hair, nods.
He clutches his poems, reams of paper, in his fists
as if they were thunderbolts, but these impotent

gifts do not catch afire, only mingle in the light
swirl of garbage stirred by the wake of a transport
careening towards Nine Miles and the fabulous Heartease.

The cryptic poems, dream messages from his fertile
brain, breeding fantastic images like nations of lice,
simply catch the wind and fly, fly, fly. His fingers

point to the turning pages, tweaking their jerk and swoop.
The anthologists and art patrons, the sober poets
who do normal things for kicks like play golf

and fantasise about infidelity, linger in the shadows
like dingoes, waiting for him to fall from fatigue,
waiting for night to gather, when they will crawl out

and collect the leaves into sheathes sandwiched
between elegiac introduction and well-researched
glossary, mapping his fall from grace.

iii

In the house there is a constant creak in the foundations
and the villagers are not sure who has died inside.
They smell the sting of pine wood and candles

and see the strangers in blacks and fanciful cars
who clot the overgrown lawn singing feebly:
"Abide with me, fast falls the eventide."

The sun wavers as if suspended on a string
over the acrylic ocean. The fence is broken and the cows
have been adopted by the neighbours, given new names.

iv

Two girls in white, immaculate like the conception,
giggle at the twitch of his buttocks, thinking
of Michelangelo's David dipped in tar and grime

with a crazy jungle of matted hair for the blond curls.
He stands there, not speaking, no longer reciting
Hopkins and praising the merit of monasteries

and the celibate life for the poet, for the soul and
spirit, the ungodding of ungod; or the merit of isolation
far from the pure adolescent white of virgin girls

who trip his eye and sweating mind each day. He no longer
grins his whiskey breath through the classroom,
pontificating, "If God wanted to come again today,

Mary would have to be ten years old!" Instead
his mouth drools; his eyes do not see; his tongue,
uncertain of itself, drags, and sometimes he snaps

at the flies like a mongrel, and the girls squeal.
First they giggle, then one recoils and falls back;
the other feels the invasion of his eyes and sobs.

v

All this we heard like a rumour whispered
by the concerned and we have heard nothing
more of him, though a collection was taken

for the roses delivered by courier to the ward.
Rumour has it he writes poems still,
on toilet paper, in his old prolific way.

The poems are all reruns: the same image,
the same turn of phrase, the same poem,
but now inverted – suddenly there is logic.

But the blaze of his irreverent magic
is gone, except for one piece, eighty lines long,
that reads, "fuck, fuck, fuck... ad infinitum".

No requiem for the poet, no martyrdom on his head,
just this quiet dozing and sleepwalking
among the crotons and white walls of the asylum.

CHAPTER XXI

The Preacher and the Prophetess Sin

i

It is Saturday night when the preacher arrives;
the wind trembles the bamboo bush
and colonnade of coconut trees; the christmas

bulbs, like multi-shaded scotch-bonnet peppers
strung on a brown wire, swing against
the purple sky. The smell of curry spices the air.

In the rumshop, the revellers bob like weed-
infested buoys, tams and head-ties just keeping
afloat over the wave of rapid-fire dancehall;

and their bodies contort and fall back into the *bogle*
while their legs flap in flamboyant *butterfly* –
Supercat dissecting the female anatomy, naming it;

Shabba giving them what they want: Flex! On
the skirts of the yard, a cluster of stoned sisters stare
to the sea swaying, expecting tomorrow to come and greet

them there, picturesque and bright. Dragon stouts in their
manicured hands, their minds slip slowly, unchecked.
They have not spoken for an hour. Empty bottles at their feet.

From the balcony, the preacherman sees the way the wind
lifts their skirts and whips them on their thighs,
the way the half-light transforms them into revelations.

These are the handmaidens of the Lord in reverie. He prophesies,
and by divine operation, their broken hymens slowly
close like the Red Sea after the tribe has passed through.

ii

Here in this yard with the earth patted firm
they gather in pew formation, facing the truth
with their backs towards the sea;

the congregation awaits the prophetess's
pronouncement. The sky is heavy,
and a red, gold and blue triangular flag

flutters in the coming chill. The thump of
the man-high speaker boxes below mainstreet
rattle the dry bamboo of the church's fence.

The sisters wait for the prophetess to electrify
like a pole in the balm yard catching the current
from the sea and then, rooted like that

in the soil of ages, to speak. She is primed,
a fresh hibiscus snug in her head-tie, her blue
frock down in modesty to her shining shins,

her head righteously tied white in deference
to the preacherman, for the power is in the channelling,
the clear path without static and pride from

God to man to woman. The congregation waits
with the curiosity of a crowd gathering around
a swelling corpse. The preacherman mutters "Nineveh"

like a curse. "O fallen village, idolatrous town,
undeserving of the flame and mercy of the prophetess's
voice" – and he wants to pull her away before she

speaks out of her tenderness. From the stronghold
of its depravity, a fat woman, in dashiki and bandana,
stares red-eyed at him, her breath, thick with the whites,

wafts defiant in the face of this coming power; he visions
the eight spirits in her twisted soul jigging to the distant
bass and drum from the rumshop down the hill.

iii

That night on the black sand
they coupled like dogs,
sweating on the shells and pebbles.

The preacher howled
and ran like a madman into the sea.
The prophetess whimpering, rested.

Then hearing his sobs amid
the pip and draw of the surf,
she gathered her gleaming nakedness, sucked

her teeth, and walked towards the cottage.
She slept in coral and shell
and woke to the yellow

of Annotto Bay's hawking,
cart-squeaking, fishmongering,
and roosters alarming.

She stretched, and rubbed
the bruise of sand-burn and pebble
on her taut buttocks

with coco-butter and cream.
Then she ate avocado and ackee
stewed in sweet coconut oil.

iv

From the second-storey window, the Bay
sprawls in olive and yellow, old
black and white nostalgia in the slow

sunset. A day has passed since the transgression,
and the prophetess's voice has carried on the wind
singing hymns of rejoicing like teasing to his ears.

The village has ignited with revival
and families have fallen at the altar,
weeping in penance. What miracles in these few hours!

The zinc roofs are strewn with bricks, stones, and twigs
tossed there by boys stoning the mango trees, and
the women, Caribbean postcards in soft focus,

wash white sheets as the curling smoke from the
small bonfires circles their bobbing heads.
The preacher, searching for his text,

sees Bathsheba in the shade of the coolie-plum tree,
sees his sermon in the prophetess sitting under
the gentle ministrations of a sister who plaits

her hair and oils the scalp. The gold of their dresses,
the glow of their shins, the mongrel scavenging for
bones nearby, all pastoral, and the preacher

turns to the word sharply, the light playing
tricks in the quiet. At this moment, this interim
before the long march through the evil street,

now slick like sin after the rain, the road moist,
the slime of the gutters stirring, the scent of bathing
trickling through the green and grime,

in this hour of sweet communion, when the spirit
will swoop off the mountains with truths for the preacher,
when the word is being birthed in his heart,

the preacherman's soul is in torment. The
prophetess fills his eyes again, silhouetted in candle-
light, her hair unleashed now, light and curling

in the caressing wind. Standing there before his eyes
discarding her garments, her ministry of shells,
naked before the congregation, soft like woman

now, her feet fermenting in the tart stickiness
of fallen sea-grapes, she sings with red open mouth,
and drawn in, he falls again and again.

It is all a dream, a vision, for she still sits in the shade,
her hair now in thick long plaits, the wind stirring
her golden skirt. The sermon is now shaping in his soul.

The prophetess waves to him from the coolie-plum tree,
and they all gather in front of the beige fence
to begin the procession of hymns and tambourines

through the village. The people follow the church
to the chapel, anticipating the spectacle of revelations.
The preacherman looks to the hills. There is no wind.

CHAPTER XXII

The Saints Return Triumphant

i

There is rejoicing in the pews this morning,
bright arcs of tambourines. The children of perdition,
faces black with the Nile's sun, are transported

in their sudden awakening to a stretch of Gaza
in the shelter of pyramids and the sphinx,
kicking up hot sand like sojourners

after the parting of the waters, after their arrival
in this fertile land of salvation. Oh, they have seen
the work of the Lord, and there is rejoicing in the pews.

There is leaping in the hall of light this morning,
spirited dancing among the saints, for the Lord
has triumphed in his holy ways, and good tidings

make their healing path through the swaying believers.
Displayed like the spoils of war, the new believers stand
in chain-link order, freshly heaved from the black water

of St. Thomas in the East. How the mighty have fallen,
how piously reverent glow these newcomers to light,
eyes still blinking, mouths still gasping for air.

ii

Myrtle, the prostitute from Annotto Bay, grins
her puss eyes, her assets concealed beneath white robes.
What magic purrs beneath the swoop of her garments?

Watch her spin like a gig unleashed, her feet blurred.
In this frenzy, all is gloriously hot; tears mingling with sweat
as Myrtle, redeemed, torments her soul on the thrashing floor.

Sandra, the nyah queen of her mountain village,
has shorn her locks and holds the long snakes
of black and silver in outstretched arms, like an offering.

Note the twitch in her tight jaw, the glaze of her eyes,
while believers gawk at this immaculate sacrifice,
as if the snakes will suddenly uncurl and attack.

Seeing, she is drinking in, gulping, her visions unleashed;
her tight neck flexes in quick spasms, as her head,
sweat clean, but unruly like the patches of a mangy bitch,

bobs and weaves, evading the jabs of the evil one.
She is skipping to the thump and syncopation of hymnals;
tongues of fire come flaming from her opened mouth.

Broad-mouthed Merle, who sprinkled her dust at the feet
of God's messenger and gathered her invisible zombies
to hurl stones from the sky while the Holy Ghost

wrought his magical glory in the twilight of the beach's
recline; Merle, whose finger could crook a grown man
to the floor, grovelling like a croaking lizard to her beck;

Merle, the power that be, poised against the wind
with her satchel of plagues and pestilence; Merle, standing in line,
captive sister of the crusading Clarice, now caught in glory,

is giddy with this new reckoning. For power like that
which she has seen at the hands of the prophetess
is power to bring supplication. These impossible occurrences,

treasured in the hearts of the people who chuckle at cynics
and their scientific quest for evidence, have brought
the heave and chaos of thanksgiving in the pews this morning.

iii

Clarice, with face glowing, as if returned
from the encounter on Mount Sinai,
oversees the rejoicing with her quick eye.

Her spoils of spiritual warfare displayed
like undulating trophies before the congregation:
he who has eyes to see, let him see.

Last Night stares stone-faced at the improbable
lauding of his exploits in battle. The congregation
translates this as the heavenly glare. None cross him.

He remembers the sting of salt, the pull of sand,
the prick of pebble and stone on his nakedness,
the sharp cold of the new wind on his startled skin;

in his throat is the howl of the madman
dashing along the fresh beach stark as birth,
waiting for the wrath to fall.

iv

She who has ears to hear, let her hear
the hallelujah chorus; see the dancing brothers,
sweat pouring, clothes sticking to their torsos,

as they leap naked in the eyes of the maidens of God:
David before Michal and her nun's pout and frown,
each leap a contest to touch Jehovah's

proffered hands. The congregation trembles
in relayed plosives, the babble of unknown tongues
washing the witnesses with impossible love.

v

Returned from the dense mist of St. Thomas in the East,
returned intact from the stronghold of Satan
and his minions of falling lights, returned unbroken,

returned triumphant, let the church say amen.
Returned with song: Can I get a witness!
Returned with feet still skipping: Glory!

Returned with captivity captive: Yes!
With the chains of degradation broken asunder: Uhuh!
With the faith intact despite the perilous way!

Returned with a song of triumph on the lips!
Returned with a song of victory on the lips!
Returned, returned, returned!

A flurry of clapping shatters the stoic resolve
of Last Night who, leaping like one unburdened,
hurls his body into the waves of fire.

Clarice, at the pulpit, collapses in her stomach
for her lover has found his feet again.
Her tears soften her path like scattered roses

at the feet of one who comes with blessings and with joy;
she gathers his broken self to her bosom
and rocks him whimpering there in the whirl of tongues.

vi

Soberly they tally the casualties and spoils of war.
Twenty saved in glorious drama; two rum-bars broken;
the obeah woman sent running; the earth rebirthing.

These are the triumphs of war. They tally the casualties
in secret: the black beach and the compulsion of flesh;
Thalbot's descent into the old madness

(cleaned like this, the demons have returned sevenfold
with deeds and squatters' rights); Thalbot fallen
to the lure of water-bellied whores.

In visions they see him beaching his broken
soul on some stone-hearted mongrel, a grotesque
image of bestial decadence. "Fallen, fallen!" laments Clarice.

"For the brilliance of blanketed miracles, secrets of the Almighty,
like the ark of the covenant and the sanctified mint of prophecy,
can blind the unchosen one, strike him dead if he sees.

Truths fed to the uninitiated sour and form ulcers.
How then could he see the ritual coupling of angels
on the black sand and not go blind with madness?"

vii

Thus saith the prophetess: "If cursed by Him,
why do I touch the broken-faced saints
and see the miracle of wounds closing?

And whose are these precise visions
of the indiscretions of the believers – these truths
on my tongue, cutting the bone and marrow

of closeted secrets? Whose are these, if not the Lord's?
If abandoned, why does the power swell in my belly
and dart in blasts of fire from my trembling hands?

Why does the spine curl, the skin shiver
in the glory of morning prayers, the bright light
of mercy startling my eyes each blessed day?

If dashed from His presence, why this constant flow
of milk from my swelling breasts at the prod
and suckle of the saints? Great is His faithfulness!"

viii

So spake the prophetess in her heart: "And now
the build-up to that abandonment of self,
to the succumbing of my limbs to the nerves'

attack, there on the black sand, Last Night
so dark and slippery in the heat.
I could only feel his straining to come

and then he was gone into the black
and the sky winked at my writhing as if
we would share this secret embrace together.

I am woman, I am blood, I am water;
I have collected, I am collecting all the rivers,
all the oceans; all the salt of the earth

seeps through my open pores. I am the songs
gathering in incredible notation around tuned
instruments, taut with anticipation,

dormant for all these years in the cloister of miracles.
Come now, says the voice from the winking sky,
and pluck her, tickle her to sing to the night.

And whose wail is this? I am a poem spoken;
each caress on my tilting body ekes a parable.
Like Sheba to Solomon's songs I bring tears;

I am comely, I am black, my watery arrivals
are testaments of ultimate love. Mythic like this,
I have departed from the temporal to the eternal,

and the clumsiness of sex, the sweat and slippery getting there –
these are mere trompings before the possession;
and then the soul is lifted beyond the wrestling.

Last Night vanished, an instrument of love, into the night
while my soul cried to the heavens.
Then I will soar – for it is flying – above the squalor of the journey.

I have seen the visions of triumphant gazelles
skipping upon the mountains, their glazed eyes
drunk with the fire of orgasmic love, constantly damp.

This coming in spasms on the black sand
is nothing but a prayer given wings;
my will usurped, I wait for His words to come."

ix

The prophecy comes without announcement.
She gets them on the toilet seat sometimes.
This time, again, it is in her mirror. She squints to see

Thalbot on the rock of pink marl, his hair grown wild,
his head filled with the secrets of her eternal damnation.
She speaks the wind from the oceans

to bring their magic of untold memories
to gather in riotous reunion in Thalbot's fertile brain.
And, as if on cue, the oceans crest and send their winds

towards the battered coast of Kingston's slums
where Thalbot is beached, waiting for night to pass
and for the cleansing of memories from his

weary mind. Clarice no longer contemplates absolutes;
the dialectics of good versus evil are now insignificant.
She misses the hubris of her swelling visions;

the elements respond to her sharp eye
and the saints gather at her door for blessings.
God is in heaven. Silent. The winds lift and move.

PART THREE

Now the word of the Lord came unto Jonah,
the son of Amittae, saying "Arise, go to Ninevah,
that great city, and cry against it; for their
wickedness is come up before me."

Jonah 1: 1-2

CHAPTER XXIII

Thalbot and the Vine

i

At the cliffs, the wind
carves its caves of eyes and gaping mouths,
the echo of last night's storm still

lingering like after-death. Thalbot hears the Lord,
"Go! Go!" He speaks in the waves and the wind,
for this is the chronicled manner of his presence.

"Go to the city where the wickedness of Sodom
is a tattered coat on their backs; you will know
them by their decadence. Tell them you have seen

the arc of my holy sceptre falling. Avoid proper
names, stick to pronouns breathed with reverence –
such aspirates from your lungs will carry fire –

this I promise. I thrive on enigma, names spoil the effect,
use symbols and pronouns. I'll do the rest.
Tell them that the light of the sky will pour

a hail of fire into their broken upturned cups.
Speak this compelling prophecy like a naked madman
in the streets and, if you must, eat grass, chew

laboriously, regurgitate, relish the green juice.
They will understand; it has been done before.
Tell them of the brilliant impossible you have witnessed

in the churchyard these last few nights, tell them
of the prospect of these truths unfolding
like a yellow banner across the dark.

I only ask that you carry my salvation
into the heart of the City." This is how the Lord
comes to Thalbot's trembling brain.

But how can he go like this, faithless
and blinded? How, after witnessing the preacherman
and the prophetess coupling like dogs on the beach?

How, after his own vicarious coming, voyeur
without the strength to look away? What is
left but this heaviness, this pull to the edge,

to the bosom of the sea where the gravel sand
and picking fish would cleanse all mortality
from his fallen flesh, where death at sea by drowning

would be cool and silent among the shell and coral?
This dying would salvage the possibility
of hope. But the voice of God is in the wind,

and visions spread across the lapping ocean in
coloured cinematic panorama. There lies the sore
of the Caribbean as midnight acolytes of worms

snake through the narrow avenues to the sound
system's call, arms tossed high in spastic animation,
the wind whipping the stench of their carelessly

dropped defecation into the air. This is the vision
spread over the ocean, and the voice of God in the wind
shouts, “Go! Go! How can you not go?”

ii

Thalbot’s reluctance is understandable.
Remember, this is his city and home,
and Bellevue, dusty and hot by the sea,

is his former residence, rising
above Seaview’s gangrened streets,
their potholes seeping brown and caking at the edge,

Bellevue, where the doctors perform casual experiments,
opening the gates of the patients’ brains
while the fans turn the sweat and farts,

circulating nothing new, just the same smells.
How to speak of salvation to the stone-throwers,
the laughing women, the teenage girls with

their startled curiosity devouring his blatant shame?
How to preach into the broken vessel where gunmen
practice marksmanship on the dizzy madmen,

and the whores urinate and spit, taking out their
resentments on the madmen’s drooping heads, as the
volvos, all rolled-up and chilling, cruise by?

Oh let the stones fall off the mountains
on this city of lapsed nyabinghi and renta-dreads.
Let old Zion fire cut through the brittle

wharfs and flame its way up the hills,
gutting the mansions and the jewelled slopes
flowering their satellites like rusting white

chrysanthemums, that catch the seed
from the Beast jerking its self-assured self
off over the Basin. This fire will leave the earth

black with nutrients and chemicals where fresh
living soil can birth new truths, new mercies.
This is Thalbot's hope, the rationale for his

flight in the other direction. For what right has a city
to live again when the prophet himself is blind,
when he has seen and cannot remove the vision

of the preacherman and the prophetess howling
in their coming? And she with her proffered bottom,
what miracle is left in the seduction of her slow

casual walk back to the chapel doors, while the
preacher tries to swallow the black ocean into his
fevered soul, sobbing like that? Fall is all. Silence

the only answer. The wind grows still, having spoken,
and Thalbot hurls the words over the sea
but they do not splash as they fall, they float.

iii

He lifts his soul and leaps over the rocks,
over the cactus and tangle of sea-grape trees
into the somnolent mainstreet, down

to the junction where a small party of travellers,
three tourists, two dreads,
and four top-flight Annotto Bay whores,

have gathered around a mini-van to journey
to Montego Bay to see Shabba and the Cat.
There is the sweet aroma of cherished colly in the air

and the van is rocking to rapid-fire synthetic
bass-lines. Negotiating his escape calmly,
Thalbot offers a red hundred dollar and climbs

into the depth of the van. One of the women
presses her softness into his side, and laughs
lightly, drawing him into the herb on her breath.

He laughs, falling into the sway of the rocking
van, the reggae trembling the loose windows.
He knows he is being watched like the sparrow.

He closes his eyes trying to forget the prophecy,
trying to quiet his bleating soul, and the van
prods its way along the coast towards Montego Bay.

iv

At Joppa the tyre explodes on a curve that
overlooks the gullied cottage of a gentle country
woman. The ferns on the hill face

drip dew; a river flowing from the rock
gurgles beneath the asphalt bridge
and spills into the lazy sea.

Disgorged in giggles and gentle expletives,
the people squat in the moonlight, eyes
glazed with the back twist of the herb,

while the driver sweats on a new wheel,
cursing at the vindictiveness of it all.
Thalbot lingers in the shadows beneath

the leaning trees, watching for careering
vehicles, or bolts of unsuspected lightning
from above. But the task is completed

without event; God stays silent. Yet, after half
a mile, the exhaust falls and clanks, the chassis
breaks, the radio falls dead, the engine sputters,

the van comes to a bawling halt, and someone
mentions a curse. As if on cue, the others
find religion and search their past for a reason.

One girl announces that she has been cursed
by her obeah grandmother, who thinks it is
church she going to now. But Thalbot knows,

hearing the spirit at his back, and sees the logic
of his truth, still too far from Tarshish.
He draws the driver aside and whispers.

He offers to walk and free them of the curse,
but the driver fears to abandon a bonafide prophet
on the road, rudderless, with no hope of salvation.

The gathering grows impatient so Thalbot
walks away. The driver shifts gear and pulls
out, the red tail-light bouncing into the blackness.

Thalbot plants his left foot and uproots the right:
the walking is tedious. He still points to Montego Bay,
leaving behind the spastic madness of Nineveh.

v

Coming with the thunder of storms,
the hiss of a whale's breathing,
this cylinder of grimy seats and caution

airbrakes, riding, caressing the sudden
curves of the wavy coastline,
the driver sweating out his quart of whites,

the blue and gold forty-seater, with
a cage of soldered iron for a crown,
sways empty in the rural night.

The broken hydraulics of the side door
flap their rhythmic metallic claps
like an alarm before the cough and rattle

of the engine. The plastic glass
of the windows rattles like shak-shaks
in the leap and lurch of this dance

threading around the potholes
of the coastline. The gear brake-down
for the turn into the hills

startles Thalbot, who is waiting at the
junction for another vessel to bear him
west before the sun breaks the horizon.

Caught in the stark light and the
slow drag of the uncertain wheels,
Thalbot stands to leap but instead

is caught in a motion as helpless as the
blind stare of a jacked deer. The air
hisses, the wheels squeal as the hiccuping

bus stops. It shudders,
nose pointed to the hills and their
enclosing trees, beyond which the roads

twist and meander, beyond which spreads
the land of Nineveh, the lamentable city,
all primed for the rain of damnation from heaven.

"You will dead out hereso, boss. Man
will cut you t'roat and drink you blood.
Come aboard. The door is open. Town!"

Looking for a light, for a village with the security
of a roadside chapel, Thalbot boards
the panting bus and looks to the

silhouette of the driver, a back,
a way of leaning against the wheel,
a texture of laughter, an omen, a prophecy.

The bus lurches and swings, the lights blink,
the shadows play games on the green
hard plastic seats; there is the smell of green bananas'

sticky blood, old thick market-sweet thyme,
the sweat of the clustered souls travelling.
Throughout those lurching hours Thalbot groans on the slopes

of twisted Mount Diablo. On the striped
and blackened steel deck lie scattered,
crushed callaloo leaves and a spill

of pepper seeds. The hills come quickly
to meet the broad windshield; the
bus sits on the road and rides it out.

Thalbot watches the comfort of country
chapels hurtle by in streaks of light,
the congregations swaying in pink hues,

the bible-bearing infants, the truth
in the steeple and bells of the facades,
but the driver, shifting gear, leaps forward.

At the top of the mountain, the glow
of Nineveh suggests itself in the sky.
Thalbot shouts to the sweating back

of the driver, but the shifting gears continue,
the blast of the horn on a chain.
The sermon in his belly sours.

The journey down into the vegetation
of the foothills is smooth, but the way
home has become uncertain.

Thalbot falls to his knees and scratches
his overheated flesh. The earth is growing
brighter in the coming dawn.

vi

"When trouble catch me, undress me,
leave me bleeding by the roadside; when
the blindness of seeing the unholy nastiness

on the beach darken me day; when the
curse of the Lord follow me from Annotto
Bay's slick street and clapping

congregation marching to the altar
and falling falling so; when the dead
arising and the cripple gyrating, and

the twist-up guava bush rejoicing;
when the prophetess riding
a new prophecy on the naked beach,

milking him, milking him;
(when last you said your prayers, woman,
when last you count your beads? Morning

coming and the thin membrane of your drying
sex will catch the sun. See the soldier crab
picking away at the charred edges) it is

the cause, it is the cause!
This my Joppa so far from Tarshish,
and a thatch and mud bed for my head,

when this duppy transport, blasting exhaust
in the air, and its coolie driver, floating on weed
an sharp whites, beckon me like a siren

and swallow me into the ribbed belly
of this steaming metal tomb, this
grave where trouble follow me. When I cry

unto the Lord t'rough what I see mek me a
soul of unclean lips and cankered eye,
who hear me cryin? Who hear me?

For when you toss me into the current,
the warm wave dem lapping lapping,
and when dead take my han, (and me,

I was not fighting,) an draw me down deep,
deep into the womb of this moist fern gully,
then drag me over the twisting road, like the coral,

black but still aglow with retained light;
when I cry out, 'Is dead a dead now!'
like a prophecy, and my eye dem see

the howling preacherman, his sex
jumping in the moonlight, his soul burning,
rolling like a madman in the water,

is dead a dead now. For what must follow
the absence of faith? What but this
seaweed like a rope round me neck,

and Albert Pierrepoint and his father and
father before him holding the lever,
ready to drop me, for the judgment of heaven

done sound on the blast of this bus.
Down, down ah falling like a bungy gone crazy,
not finding the jolt, just air; down,

down Mount Diablo, to Flat Bridge, to
Maroon jungle-green, the Rio Cobre,
slipping its hiss, quiet as water, me

waiting for the whiplash, the wail,
the crack, the coolie man swaying now,
spliff after spliff giving him

a heavenly cloud. When falling like this,
who it was that bear me up,
bring me forward still breathing?

This journey stop before the Baptists' Cathedral
front a Parade lignum vitae shade.
Who but the Lord coulda plan the path

to this holy temple, the wind beating through
my open mouth? Yes, Father, see me here,
flat, eating the shit and dirt, eating grass.

Free me up, Giver, and Thalbot will find
music, abandon the flesh, the madness,
drop me foot and preach. You see my card now.

Though it sound like rejoicing for miracle
what done realise, this is a transaction. You see
my collateral; take it or hang me, Giver. Amen!"

vii

And the Lord commanded the bus
and it vomited Thalbot onto dry land;
and the city grunted, then turned over.

The bus rattled around the Parade Square
saluting Marcus and the fat queen,
then vanished like magic into its own tail-smoke.

viii

On the beach, the sisters shoulder the soil,
falling back like limboing captured warriors on the slaver's
deck, Madonna brassieres instead of blouses on their backs,

as with martial precision, the arms
windmill in slow molasses motion,
the lips pout, eyelids droop

bogling rough on the beach with *festival*
pipping in the dutch pan, and snappers
pinking in the onion and pepper seed.

Riding like this, feet planted in the sand,
batty-riders exposing the jelly buttocks,
pum-pum printers declaring the goods fresh,

their sweat drips and is sucked in by the sand,
as Supercat in a fancy white tux
slicks his hair back with a coolie glow.

Thalbot's prophecy gathers under the yellowing
frond of the toxin-drunk coconut trees. Thalbot
opens his palms releasing the words like

a runaway kite and then, with a prayer
of benediction, his voice tries to battle the surf
and raggamuffin. He falls silent, supplanted

by the women butterflying on the beach.
The close-up camera discourses its own hell.
The wind falls. The curse is earnest now.

ix

Thalbot walks by the cactus and blackened bush
along the broken shore strewn with gleaming tyres,
the rusting husks of discarded vehicles, wrinkled

where the impact was sudden; and barefoot and naked
like this, his hair rediscovering the familiar path
of tangle and unruly knots, he will howl like a jackal

and moan like the owl perched there on the male
guinep tree, all frills and bursting foliage, yet barren:
a bearded woman straining for respect in the sun.

"If a liar and deceiver comes and says,
'I will prophesy for you plenty wine and beer,'
he would be just the prophet for this people.

If a sweetmouth songmaker come and chant,
"I will prophesy for you nuff visa and volvo,'
he would sit in a high seat among the leaders.

If a stone rise up from the marl pits
and declare apples, grapes, jingling money
for your pockets, you would call it god."

x

From the cove of marl on Edgewater coast
the ospreys dive seaward; a slow blackened
cargo liner trundles across the blue.

Planes disappear in their landing
behind Palisadoes trees, the cylinders
shimmering. This vista of the soap factory

and its smoking towers, the wharfs, blue and rusting,
layered like Aztec gardens, is the barrier
between the stinking Dungle and the healing

sea. Thalbot fasts till white lines his lips
and the edge of his eyes. The sun is steady
in the rock bay. The salt lips the edge.

Snails lock into the wet grey stone.
The smells carry faster across the water
than sound. But Thalbot shouts anyway.

The waves, barely presenting themselves, carry
his voice for a few yards and then all goes flat.
The cactus, the salt-stiff bramble, the brier

of the stony path to this sanctuary are dry.
The white rocks are stained with the blood of
Thalbot's broken feet. Praying now, he dreams.

xi

The congregation rests in the silence of the praying.
Clarice's eyes see the spin of John crows
over the discarded skyscraper, abandoned

seashore resort leaning over a beach that looks
like mud, the impromptu jetty where naked boys
dive into a stagnant pool.

Clarice visions Thalbot naked on the rock face,
lusting, his member clutched in his spittle-slick
fist. She declares it to the believers, omitting

only the most vulgar of details: the white, the surf,
the exclamations of his coming. She presents the
coordinates of his shelter, however, and declares him

reprobate. The congregation will pray, but some,
she knows, will seek him out to gather their stones
and smash him bloody into the white pink marl

Clarice pricks Last Night the preacherman to add his
truth, this man who since the night on the beach
has become a useless rag. He rises and curses

Thalbot's inconsistency and disobedience, declares him
mad. He turns to Clarice whose bosom heaves,
the imprint of her nipple obvious to him.

They deny the falsehood of the rumours of their
coupling. Evildoers like Thalbot filled with envy,
they explain, and the congregation sighs amen.

xii

"I have spoken the prophecy like you asked me,"
complains Thalbot. "Now you hear what they are
saying of me? Hear the laughter negating me!"

The sun beats black into Thalbot's naked back
as he labours in the government garden
swinging his machete there in the Kishon Valley,

and the petals flutter, sheered chrysanthemums,
orchids, roses, dandelions broken in the growing gloom
and the sun, startled, gathers its cloak and flees.

Left to bleed, the severed stems droop
over the bed of fading petals, and from the sea
a cloud, small as a man's fist, comes towards land.

After this execution, when the sign of the flame
(and maybe a hint of vindictive anger)
offered up the sacrifice of these

government-funded prophets, Thalbot
stands over their corpses with his slick bright machete
dripping, hanging from his righteous hand.

"It is done," he prays. "It is the cause. It is the cause."
He tries to find the corpse of Clarice in the heap
but finds nothing blue with red flaming lips.

From the greenhouse and gardener's shack
at the end of the park, the bearded custodian
screams towards Thalbot with a windmilling rake;

Thalbot sprints towards the coast, and finds
shelter in the cove where he stares into the silk
of the evening sea. The fist has come and rested on his soul.

The silence of the Lord torments the prophet.
His eyes see only the glimmer of the sea.
There, beneath the broom tree, he rests.

xiii

The clatter of the wind can be heard
deep inland. The boats reel and dip;
some tip and come up sputtering.

This is no camouflaged, covert wind
trying to enter alien airspace without fanfare;
this wind carries the clank and clash

of broken metal and creates its own alarm,
promising the uprooting of trees, the hurling
of vehicles, the destruction of homes.

When it comes it carries rain like stones
which shatter the marl-stone quarry
where Thalbot is sheltered and the wall

gives way like crumbling cheesecake. The people
brave the elements to witness this single-minded
wind whipping its electric tail back and forth,

blasting the rockface to dust. It goes nowhere else.
And there, where the tractors lie idle, a tombstone of
precious ochre marl jutting sharply, the gaping claw

of the mechanical spade drips clumps
of dark transported soil and stone, like a wounded
boxer bleeding from every orifice.

The children of this wicked generation do not
hear the naked prophet as he howls into the wind,
rejoicing. Nor do they hear his gloating.

In the swirl of this visitation, Thalbot cannot see
the way the wind repeats its assault on the rock
sheltering him, so he thinks this fist now turned

in on the island will ride the alleys, Marcus Garvey Drive,
Mandela Highway, Beverly Hills, the high and by-ways,
wreaking vengeance on the banana trees, the cane, the buildings,

the lignum vitae, the ticking zinc roofs, the sound
systems, the arrogant steeples of the churches:
the earth itself will fall like this mountain.

He is dancing and spinning in the blast, for after
so much fasting, after all that shame and lamentation,
the Lord is whipping his tail and speaking.

But the wind uncurls its fist and spreads
its impotent, caressing fingers into a breeze
as it tickles the tears of the kneeling onlookers

and shudders a weary coconut tree; then,
going to the hills, it turns into a cloud of mist
and lands in dew on the green leaves and grass.

In this sudden vacuum, Thalbot's wail sounds
into the Edgewater bungalows, his arms spread,
his eyes giving their last passion of tears, and then

his diaphragm falls with his naked body
into the marl and dust of the mountain.
He does not weep, does not laugh, does not

howl anymore, just sits there lamely,
numb to the slight drizzle. And when God
speaks, the voice echoes off Thalbot's forehead.

xiv

This mesh of vine – one vine – that finds its own anchor
twirled around its own branch, tail swallowed
by flowering head, this course-maker finding

its own path, leaf on leaf, lapping like lattice,
bars the sun, rain and dust of the marl
pit. Freshly growing, it shelters Thalbot's

dazed body leaning on its own pivot; no words,
just the back silent towards the sky
as the seagulls spill their nourishment

onto the stone and dirt. At first Thalbot resists
but the pain of his stomach is too much.
So he eats without relish, grudgingly, the rhythm

of a prisoner doing what he must. The mesh
of leaves tickles his taut skin stretched like a drum
with no hands to beat out a new prophecy.

This cool canopy of God's goodness
is an offence that he grows used to,
and out of idleness he carves his initials

into the twisted branches. At the protruding roots
he patterns the sea bed with a landscape
of pink-blue shells and smooth pebbles.

This is his mocking shrine – now defiant artist –
to ungod. This his unspoken offence to
the seeing eye. This his stone in the good God's

face. The sky is shattered, a broken mirror,
and the silence grows wide on the turning
ocean. This before the wind tries to speak again.

He has looked for the surreal of ladders
bringing down from the clouds to the sea
some visitation. But there is no traffic.

Soon colonies of worms crawl towards his shelter
and multiply in squalid sexuality until
they carpet the shelter with their convulsions.

Resigned to this revelation, Thalbot
lays his head back and crosses his arms
waiting for the canker to set in. But the worms

ignore him in their single-minded march
to the root and leaves of the vine, his shelter.
They yellow the vegetation, perforating the leaves.

It is quick and complete this destruction.
Thalbot glances upward, wincing at the sudden light.
"My home, too? Is this your idea of a joke?"

In Kingston's orange glow, the worm swallows
its last morsel and the gutter closes like a grave
on another corpse, daily slaughtered souls,

the incidental deaths of a cursed city,
disease of the indiscriminate gun, the wheeling machete,
the glass and crunch of cars colliding.

The eye of God, cyclops in the dusk, winks.
"Kill me now! Take my soul for I have no reason
to live longer! Kill me now, then drown this city."

The light fades in ribbons of pink on an orange
fabric turning red and, despite the heartfelt
prayer of Thalbot, now in despair, Kingston

has not fallen yet. So soft is the hand of the Lord,
so slow its descent upon the wayward, so gentle
his wrath. The pocked squalor of Rio still thrives

and Port au Prince's upper classes rejoice in their
long-preserved decadence, despite the dry bed and
sewer-bearing rivers. The White House still glimmers

despite the amassed dead, despite the gutted ghettos,
holes like track marks needled into tender flesh.
In the old days judgment was swift. Think of

Port Royal, now buried, her broken houses like
tombs on the white sea bed, silver darting blades
tunnelling in and out of the blind sockets of

the sunken generation. Thalbot languishes
in the skeletal remains of his shelter, without words,
without the light of revelation. Broken like this he weeps.

XV

When the charred raven comes with meat in its beak,
slanting against the sun, Thalbot stones it
and the thud sends it sudden down to the rock.

The heat cooks the fresh meat and the ants
gather quickly. The bird's beak bleeds and dries;
then the flies dance around its moist rectum.

Underneath the twigs and lattice aridity of his
drought and worm-ridden arbour, Thalbot hears
Clarice's panting like bloody Jezebel calling him down

to the rocks. The mongrels catch the scent
of death while she is falling from the wall. Clarice
has prophesied his dying; the congregation rises

for the reading-out. Thalbot sees all this in his
quiet dozing; the dogs' jaws snap at flies
as their lazy eyes stare into the broken belly,

the viscera and warm blood of the fallen
Clarice. The raven's silver-black feathers
flutter slightly in the breeze. Thalbot weeps

for the prophecy he cannot speak, this curse
upon him, the path of disobedient prophets
now stuck with powerless clairvoyance.

The seer tongue, once fire,
now damp coals,
has lost the will to speak.

PART FOUR

If my land cries out against me
and all its furrows are wet with tears,
if I have devoured its yield without payment
or broken the spirit of its tenants,
then let briers come up instead of wheat
and weed instead of barley.

Job 31: 38-40
New International Version

CHAPTER XXIV

Speaking for the First Time

"To speak my words would be to fracture
the wings of a myth and send it careering
to the sun-baked earth." So said the prophetess.

"To speak this now would be to shatter
the brittle wing-bones of a myth. To speak this
now after the long silence, after the vow to keep

the tongue arrested, cleaving to the palate;
to speak this now, having been
written into a fist of power, a magical

construct with the punch of a saint;
to speak now after the holy elders have
gathered at my feet as to a goddess and presented

their offerings, their exposed hearts and secret sins,
the crumpled hundred dollar bills, the funky
handkerchief of some clandestine affair,

the poured olive oil, the fragrance and herbs,
the delicate minds teetering at the abyss,
the hunger, the dread of the creditor's knock;

to speak this now after the whore's hymen
has been so carefully sealed, after the stone has
been removed and the three day dead has stumbled forth,

after the impossibility of miracles has been chronicled,
after I have been written into myth, into character
and role model, now player, now closed icon;

to speak this now, to empty my heart to the wind,
my mind that I have forgotten, lobotomised, without
motive, without fear or frailty, without sex;

to speak this now, talking woman, gossiping
herstory, to burst the straining dam, to rebel
against the white robe of righteousness and the tightly

girded loins; to speak thus, in a voice that deconstructs
the metalanguage of God's clever narratives, would be
to fracture the vulnerable wings of a myth.

But the air is too thin here at the gate of Heaven,
and I am tired of waiting in line despite the order
of my papers, when below me the clouds beckon.

How I have longed to fall through and feel the amassed
cool of dew drops, first rain on my living skin;
to let my hair snarl its unruly self in the fingers

of the wind; to let fall, my skirt billowing,
revealing the muscle and flesh of my thighs,
the embroidery of white nylon twined in the silver

of my pubis. I am discarding the visa to heaven,
unlocking the tongue of my imprisonment,
despite Peter's frown and the stares of the pilgrims.

But they always knew of my secret fantasies
in the pink and powder of my jewelled cage;
they all saw the red bubble of my indiscretions,

the grunt and sigh on the black beach in Annotto Bay.
The visa was a simple act of payola from the gracious
brothers whose secrets I carry in my fevered head.

So now, I fall, giving myself up for dead
and not giving a damn who goes down with me.
Now broken, my wings limping, I gladly fall,

for my mouth explodes at the rush of sound,
words tumbling forth in the thick smell of earthly
truths, tongue running wildly, shaping words,

flowering in the new sun. Falling thus, the lewd sibilants,
the orgasmic gutturals, the round voluptuous vowels:
myth falling, myth falling. It is exhilarating!"

CHAPTER XXV

Miracles

I hear voices in my head.
It happens when I least expect.
I am crossing the garden to the tomato bed.

Then arresting me, the voice
says its piece: "Tanya needs four
hundred to service her vice."

And I get the tomato,
slice the soft skin
and feel my face glow.

CHAPTER XXVI

The Perks of Prophecy

This morning, a boy looked away from my eyes
because he thought I could see into his heart.
He was right: I was naked there. But I did not speak it.

Tonight, the Spirit, I know, is grieved;
something like jealousy in his stony silence.
I confess the boy's stammering eyes made me smile.

I did flirt with his shamed soul, warming inside at the power.
How could I reprimand him for his lusting of me?
Flattered, I let him go. It's my little indulgence. Sue me!

CHAPTER XXVII

The Last Poem

... For us, all there is is trying. The rest is not our business...

(Paraphrasing Eliot)

This I heard, perhaps in a dream,
but I hoped it was the voice of God
easing up some on my burdened soul.

But it came not like the wind off the hills,
nor did the sky flame with the bloody cypher
of his finger. This was no nick-of-time bleat

of a sent ram in the thicket. Alas
these were the words of a dead poet,
with no evidence of salvation, no backative,

no promise of returns and blessings for obedience,
just the poet's flirtations with the cadence
of a god. So I sat among the roses

and chewed at the bitter leaves. The weight
of the Lord's commanding drooped my
broken head, and the leaves of the slim

volume of verse, this quartet, this clandestine fantasy, this hope
for the power of earth-makers, stone-breakers,
rustled insignificantly and impotently like a poem.

CHAPTER XXVIII

Flight

i

And when I die, I will fly. What promises you have for me?
Call it a bargain basement faith, but I have to find
something what can fit my broad hip and match my

complexion. What you have for me? When I die
my pains will be no more; I will touch clouds
damp with next week's storms, over

the cedars and pines, above the smooth green
thighs of the Blue Mountains and, when I dip like a bucket,
the water from the rocks will be cool blue.

My watertight goatskin satchel will carry
smooth stones, cooling pebbles for under my tongue
when the harmattan dries the Atlantic

air waves. I will fly over Cuba
and say a prayer for Fidel (stroking my chin), for
despite the bad press, defecting daughters, etcetera, I dig

the man for his cynic's wit and mannish ways. Look the
boat-load of criminals he liberate on Miami's
red, white and oil-blue shore, and see how blood flow –

sangre de dios – in the palmetto beachhead when each defectee
prance the golden roads with scar-face badness,
dusting the green with coke like wedding rice.

Though hesitant, I will pit-stop over Babylon,
in some third world barrio like South Carolina's low country
or them turtle-green islands where they preserve

the tongue of Africa, lodged in seed and stomach,
static magic swirling on Sycorax's fantastic Bermudes,
where black man Caliban still howls his panting heart.

Then it's east, for the cold bite hugging too tight
the Atlantic rocks. East it is, for this soulful flight,
looking, looking for soil to plant in – looking, sniffing.

East along the channels of air, warm Gabon air,
smelling the *akra*'s mellow smoothness, the sweet
kelewele, calling, calling, drawing me along the warm

currents. I'm flying east for the fleshpots
of Cairo, the sphinx, the pyramids – not home,
just legacies of gifts we have left, simple skeletons.

There on Cairo's streets, panoramas of faces
whip by like old statues of ancient times,
while the Black American intellectuals sip sweet coffee

in the cafes, retrieving their lost heritage in the coloniser's
tongue. Ah, the relics of our lost histories, the things
we have lost – seeking out a Black Atlantis so far, so far

from the conclave of huts and the circle of the griot's music
in the south, where green explodes in mountains
rising out of the brittle grit and dust of the Sahara.

Whitewashed memories are shored up in colourful texts
and clichés of a glorious race. Divided is Africa;
the Egyptians wince at the kente and dashiki.

Fly, I must, from this museum of broken dreams;
fly, I must, south to the antiphonal howls of the
Mahotella Queens, the magic of the Mokola daughters,

the flaring nostrils of the township shabeens,
speaking easy their histories in the firelight;
their eyes staring far like the Masai's gaze.

This is my dignity, this my familiar earth, this my arrival,
still damp with the dew of tomorrow's rain.
I alight without fanfare from the blue; the earth

reaches up its red fingers and sucks me, legs first,
deep into the blooming bottom-land. This yank
tautens my neck like a kite rope, my head a dignity flag.

This is my dignity, constructed by so many journeys.
Why must I stay satisfied with rumours
of old women's proverbs and the *brujo*'s sharp

recognition of healing in each weed, bush and turning
leaf? Return I must to that old shrine, now broken,
for those left behind forgot to feed the soil.

Shrine of my deepest fears, whose fingers reach
across the centuries and touch my eyes, my offspring
wrestling with the Holy Ghost found in the mountain chapel;

shrine of my deepest fears, split in my devotion
from the earth that beckons me with her smell of seed
to the new libation of blood shed for remission of sin;

shrine of my deepest fears, have you not heard that I wept
and felt the fingers on my cheek wiping, wiping;
that I have dreamed of another land, comely, home?

shrine of my deepest fears, path to my distant time,
not that path which would find me back in Jericho,
or as nigger Simon on Golgotha staring at the black sky;

shrine of my deepest fears, what wind is blowing now
to meet my uneasy mind? I feel the travail in my bones.
What do you have to offer, dare I fall open before you?

Then, land I have heard about,
will you rise before my face from the spread
of desert and thick bush, Kilimanjaro

probing the cloud cover? Is this my
Eden, my heaven? Have you something better?
Have you a truth to plant me like a tree?

ii

Culture is flux. Flux is culture. Absolute spirit.
Is spirit absolutely true? Heart is not history. Heart of stone.
Heart is the fire caught-up within my bones.

Heart is prophecy frothing to the stomp and rattle
of the gospeller's Sunday. Heart is the word spoken
so deep in the stomach, so jealously protective of my soul.

Heart is my eye peering into our collective pasts
and, finding that ancient shrine in some broken hut,
drawing me. I arrive a stranger. I arrive dead. Sleep

never comes easy, for the trees of the mountain sanctuary
rustle their hymns, calling me back, calling me back.
Flux is culture. Culture is flux. We are changing inside.

iii

The dashiki I wear is a flag.
Calls me dignified. The kente, a gift
from the Ghanaian attaché, my banner.

The sandals and the dust, my contact
with the earth. There is no burden of guilt
in my history; I will not share the blame for the callous

whip; the gospel of enslavement,
justified sardining of humanity
in our own juices, value packaged

and shipped with the blessing and guiding eye
of the all-seeing papal man; nor for the stolen gold;
the satchel of smallpox and rude disease;

the blood spilt; the betrayal and slaughter of Toussaint;
Sam Sharpe bleeding in the cane fields;
the dangling of Bogle; the black and white churches;

the rejected cornerstones falling, falling in the
black water of your hell; the silencing of my songs.
I will not be no beast of burden for you no more.

I reject twilight schizophrenia; illusions
of white Jesus with his red heart
enshrined in thorns, and his hippie

hair smoothly permed as he stands propped by
his Anglo disciples with thin, stiff upper lips;
I reject, too, the Academy of Regret;

your constant belief in the beauty and joy
of Colon's accidental landing; the perpetual admonition
to avoid the backward glance for your sake;

as if it were I facing the judgment
of salt and fire, as if I had left nothing
of beauty in the old village by the sea.

No, I will not deny the prophet with
wicked locks and a Trench Town bob
in his rhygin walk who says look back,

for that yoke is easy and the burden light,
and our legacy is more than the homelessness
of the sea – I have planted seed and it has sprouted

in this new soil, I have wailed to the hills
and my voice has returned dew soft
with clear melody and the harmony

of new trees, new brooks, new light;
the antiphonal prayers of old bones
calling me to take shelter in the green.

So there's nothing strange here;
nothing odd in my ancient garb,
and the path of my metaphors.

You have, I know, heard it all before,
and more sweetly spoken, I am sure;
but I repeat the litany to clear the table

so we may start afresh. Now, clean as I am,
plealess; now that we know the lay of the land,
offer me what you have for me – go on. I am listening.

You see, I've always known this stuff –
this stuffing of history – to be
the baggage of your sterile sermons;

secretly concealed behind those curtains
while you down the best part of the wine
after we've just dipped and sipped small;

behind your Oxford tongue, acrobatic
around that clean sermon of bloodless salvation;
locked up in some closet, all this stuff

is sitting there, and if it wasn't for that smell,
that thick muggy smell seeping through,
I would never know you had all this stuff.

iv

I have come like this to see you point me
out in my cloth from Togoland and my
raggamuffin gait. Finger me now, I don't

give a damn who sees. I won't cause no
trouble. Tell the ushers to stay cool. I will smile
'cause I come to find a path – and this won't be

a path you make, it will be a path you may offer,
then I will decide and either walk the asphalt
or ride the cobalt sky on that chartered journey back.

See me sometime as your old black ancestor
before Peter at the door, proffering her
letter of recommendation to be relayed up

the ladder to God's desk or to his well-paid
letter writers: the risen popes, paul, newton, augustine
of the burning groin. Like her, I come

like a comma to replace the closure
of your periods, screwing up the text
until the end is somewhere in the middle.

Now, tell me, what you have for me,
for this Sowetan gum-boot dancer,
this Akan mother transported like a scroll,

discovered here where the bush still parts
for her footfall, slowly marching
from the sea inland to the sound of the drum?

What you have to offer me to break this miasma
of uncertain homes? What promises can speak above
the smell clamouring behind the curtains?

You see, the path you raise your left finger to
is a false path, o false prophet. This I have
seen. My morning songs lift me beyond

the chaos of your many and twisted roads.
Flying comes so natural to me these days
as I ride this sun-full, misty morning to Heartease.

v

I am reluctant to leave it like this;
the tricks, the sin, the betrayals, as if this was all.
My journey has drawn me astray and, remiss,

I am turning to the old songs. Marley's call
from the darkness is pure light and hope
despite the countless dead by unbelief.

This song has wallowed in its grief
as if there was no music in the bright aftermornings,
no prayer caught in the mist's delicate sieve.

Now, rising up like a fisherman's weighted seine
to God, the tambourines celebrate the joy of faith rewarded,
the sickly child awakening after prayer,

sight returned to a warped cornea,
hope in a miracle of a child born intact.
How green is the island when it rains!

This song has lamented like a spoilt child,
yet how can I turn from these miracles
without tears of thanksgiving in my eye?

I write these poems with trepidation,
as if this tantrum might bring down the wrath
of the Almighty. But the prophets no longer groan

through the stinking city. Their feet skip on the mountains.
The cleansed are dancing on the hill's broken path.
Now, there is laughter and belief in mornings.

ABOUT THE AUTHOR

Born in Ghana in 1962, Kwame Dawes moved to Jamaica in 1971 and spent most of his childhood and early adult life in Jamaica. He is a writer of poetry, fiction, nonfiction, and plays. As a poet, he is profoundly influenced by the rhythms and textures of that lush place, citing in an interview his "spiritual, intellectual, and emotional engagement with reggae music." He is the author of seventeen collections of poetry, two novels, several works of creative non-fiction and the editor of many anthologies.

He is currently the Glenna Luschei Editor of *Prairie Schooner* at the University of Nebraska, where he is a Chancellor's Professor of English and a Coordinator of the UNL Creative Writing Program, a faculty member of Cave Canem, and a teacher in the Pacific MFA Program in Oregon. He is co-founder andprogramming director of the Calabash International Literary Festival, which takes place in Jamaica in May of each year and is the director of the African Poetry Book Fund. In 2018 he was elected as a Chancellor of the Academy of American Poets.

ALSO FROM PEEPAL TREE

Jeremy Poynting
Kwame Dawes' Prophets: A Reader's Guide
ISBN: 9781845234133; pp. 297; July 2018; £12.99

This guide is written from the conviction that *Prophets* is a major work of Caribbean poetry, and that whilst it can be read with enjoyment without the aid of a book of this kind, it is a work so rich in local reference and allusion that a little help can enhance the reader's understanding and pleasure. The first part of the book, a critical commentary discusses *Prophets* in its social and political setting of 1980s Jamaica, the significance of the poem's social geography; and perhaps most necessarily, it elucidates the poem's religious context, in particular, how it relates to both Biblical and Jamaican notions of prophecy and to the theology of the emergent Charismatic churches. It discusses *Prophets*' relationship to the key texts that influenced it, or against which it was written, including Derek Walcott's *Omeros*, Sylvia Wynter's *The Hills of Hebron* and the early novels of Alice Walker and Toni Morrison. The first part concludes by discussing *Prophets*' formal excellencies as a poem, and the themes and tropes that both give it coherence and make it an important work in the postcolonial cannon. The critical commentary also discusses the important role that allusion plays in the poem and its conscious riskiness as a communicative device.

The second part of the book provides chapter summaries and line by line annotations to the poem. These include notes to references to specific social and cultural manifestations of 1980s Jamaica, to places mentioned in the poem, and above all to the poem's many allusions: to the Bible and to other works of literature, and also to the reggae lyrics that locate the Bible and the prophetic in Jamaican popular culture.